# *Pattern*

# *Perfect*

# A COLORING BOOK FOR ADULTS

Other Adult Coloring Books by I. Nita Color:

Mandala Mania!

Kaleidoscope Crazy

An Abstract Mind

Mandala Mania 2

Through the Glass: More Kaleidoscope Images

# *Pattern*

# *Perfect*

## A Coloring Book for Adults

### BY I. NITA COLOR

# Table of Contents

Welcome to the world of adult coloring books!

When I was a girl, I *loved* to color! I still do. In fact, as I've gotten older I've discovered that I don't just *want* to color – I *need* to color! (Get it? I. Nita Color? Thought you might.)

If you've been bit by the creative bug and just started rediscovering coloring books, it can be a bit overwhelming. In fact, as I studied reviews of coloring books, different kinds of pens, pencils, erasers and accessories, I got a little overwhelmed *for* you! There are so many options out there! Wax pencils, oil-based pencils, alcohol-based pencils, markers of every shade, shape and imagined color, erasers that retract, erasers that don't, mineral spirits, paper stubs …

*Whoa!* I though. *All I want to do is color! All I need to learn is just enough to get other people started, too!!*

Feeling my sense of bewilderment?

Fear not! Coloring is still fun! You don't need to get so caught up in the details of *how* to do this that you miss the joy of just sitting down, picking up a colored pencil or pen and *doing* it. I'm going to tell you a couple of basics. Anything else you need to know, glance over at YouTube, ask a friend or visit a craft store and track down a store rep. They'll be happy to give you pointers and steer you toward the coloring tool you desire.

For now …

The kind of pencil you use seems to be more a personal choice than a measurable one. Many professional artists use a combination of oil- and wax-based pencils, and add some watercolor pencils and other mediums as they seem appropriate.  In other words, don't sweat the small stuff!

If you're just starting out, you can begin with a Crayola colored pencil set of 64, or go a step up to an artist-grade pencil. The most popular brands are the PrismaColor Premier Set (72 or 120 pencils) and the DeWert Artist Pencils (72 colors). These pencils are sold in sets or individually, making it easy to replace used colors as needed. I began with the Crayola option and began to replace used colors with the more expensive, longer lasting and better quality artist-grade pencils as colors ran out. I'll be purchasing individual oil-based pencils soon, just to find out if I like them better and see how they blend and combine with my old favorites.

If you use pencils, wax, oil or any other, you'll need a good pencil sharpener. Don't be cheap when it comes to your sharpener! Make sure you buy one that has a long blade (short ones break your lead) and save those shavings! The colors can be mixed with water or solvent to use as a background color for your images.

You may also choose to invest in a blender pencil, which allows you to ... well, to blend colors. While there are techniques to blend without a blender pencil, these tools can be quite useful. Some techniques will be covered below.

Waxed pencils create 'bloom', or pencil dust. I always blow it off my images and, usually, that works. However, you might want to buy an inexpensive cosmetic brush to be a little more precise in bloom removal.

You can also use colored markers when coloring. All coloring books I produce are one-side-only pages, saving the issue of bleed-through ruining an image you'd planned on coloring. Like pencils, markers come in a wide variety of styles and colors. Look for a brand that offers a fine-tip and an ultra-fine tip. As with pencils, Crayola offers a great box of beginner-level markers. They come in a box of 50 and can be slowly replaced with higher quality marker when you see that this hobby is one you plan to pursue.

Make sure your pencils are very sharp before you begin coloring and be prepared to sharpen them often during your project. Don't be afraid of being bold with your colors! While subtlety is important, vivid colors make an image pop. Know that building up layers of colors is a great way to combine and enhance them. Color in small circles, holding your pencil at an almost vertical angle. You may choose to lay down a base coat of black or white before you begin coloring a n image, automatically making it darker or brighter as you layer your intended color on. Keep your strokes nice and neat, trying to avoid a scribble look.

Mix colors for a deeper, natural look. Plan ahead what colors will go well together and enhance your picture. Lay down a solid coat of the first color, then come back in with one or more other colors on top of the foundation. Use pressure to change shades slightly, but don't put it on too thick. You can also use a blending pencil or pen to really meld the colors together when your layering is complete.

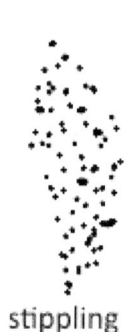

stippling

Many images won't need a lot of different techniques to give you a great finished picture. Some, however, will be enhanced by different drawing techniques and, besides, they're fun to experiment with!

Stippling is created when a series of small dots are place in the picture.

**Stippling** is usually used to indicate shadow, but can also create motion within a picture. If you use stippling to enhance the shadowing of a picture, you may still wish to use darker shade beneath it to give it even more depth. Keep all the shadowing on the same side of individual parts of a picture to make it seem real.

**Hash marks** are also a way to slightly change the appearance of a picture. Hash marks are created by making a grid that run at a diagonal. They may vary in thickness and be in colors that compliment or contrast the image you're placing them over.

Another technique is the use of indentions. Place the image on top of a piece of FunFoam or several layers of newspaper. With a black ballpoint pen, trace each line in the image, pressing hard to indent the paper. The slight variation to the surface of the paper will create more interest in the completed project. You may also create indentions within the image you'll be coloring by using a pen or pencil that matches the paper color (in this case, white). Place your image over the padding as described above and draw spirals, hash marks, geometric shapes or whatever you desire on the inside of a segment of your picture. When you color the segment, the indention will appear l, although just slightly.

There is certainly more to know about coloring books and adult coloring! You'll find several hours worth of videos on YouTube, a barrel full of blogs and pieces in the traditional media about coloring as an adult. You can always access these resources if you have questions or contact us on (you guessed it!) our Facebook page.

But for now, grab a marker or pencil … Ready, set, color!

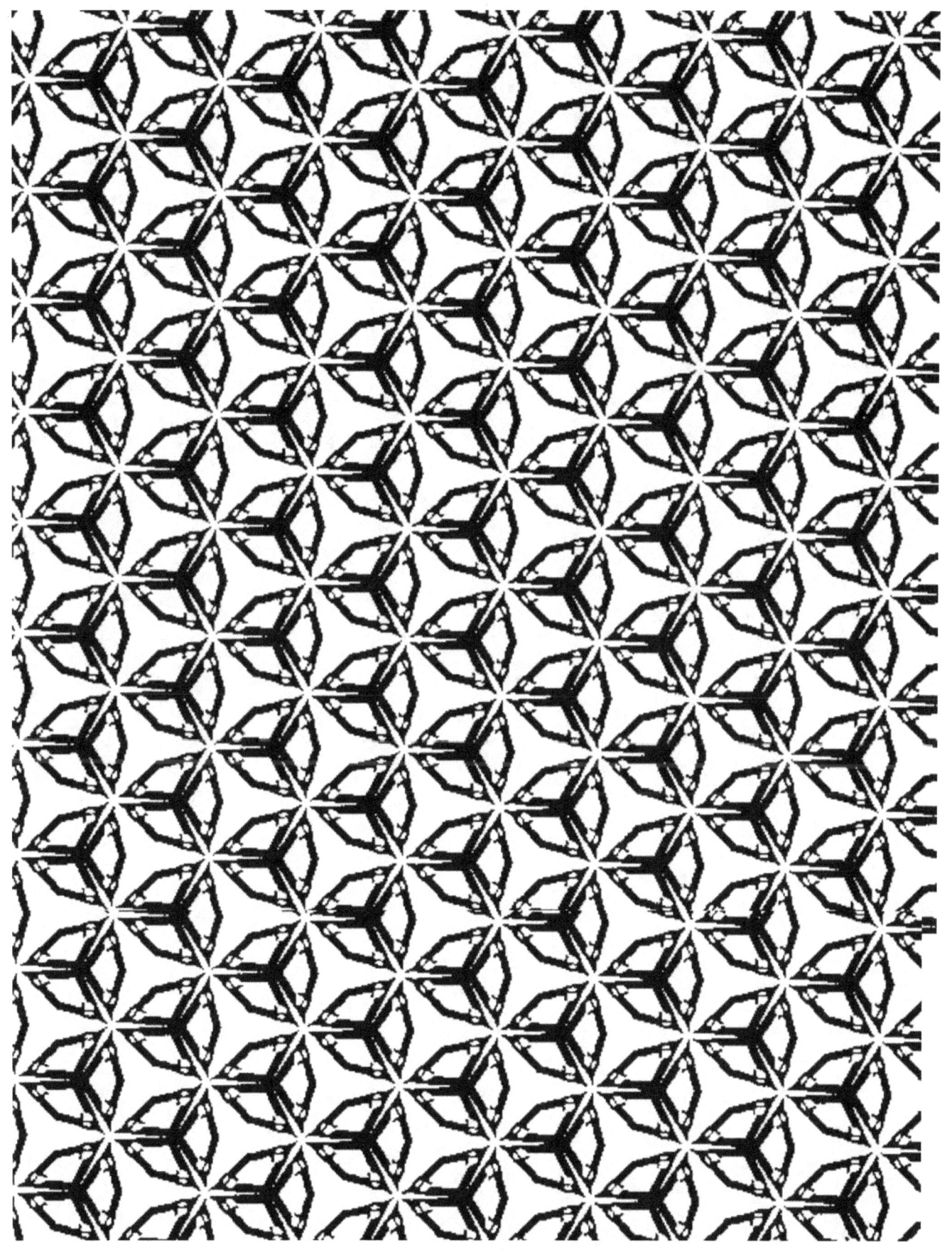

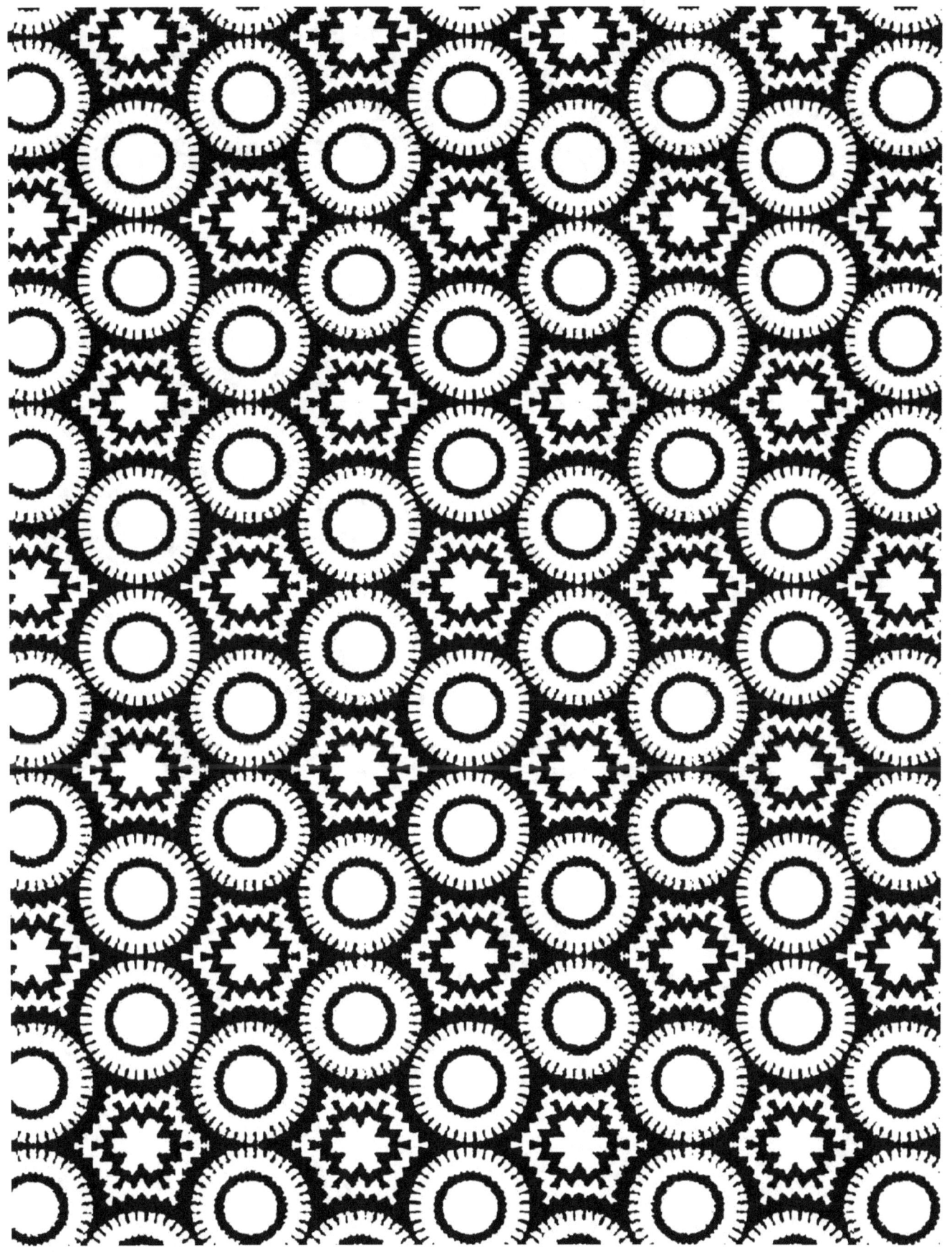

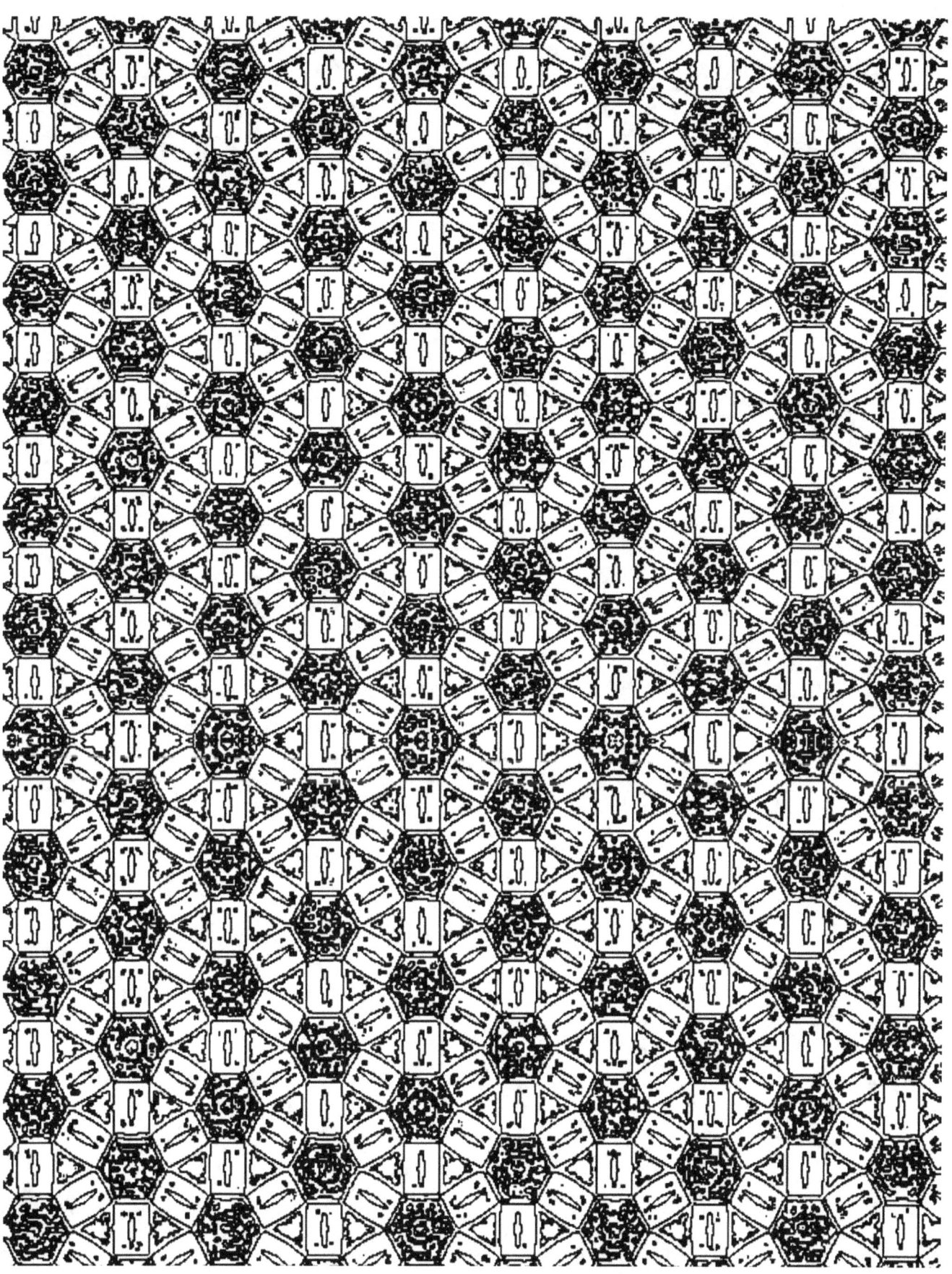

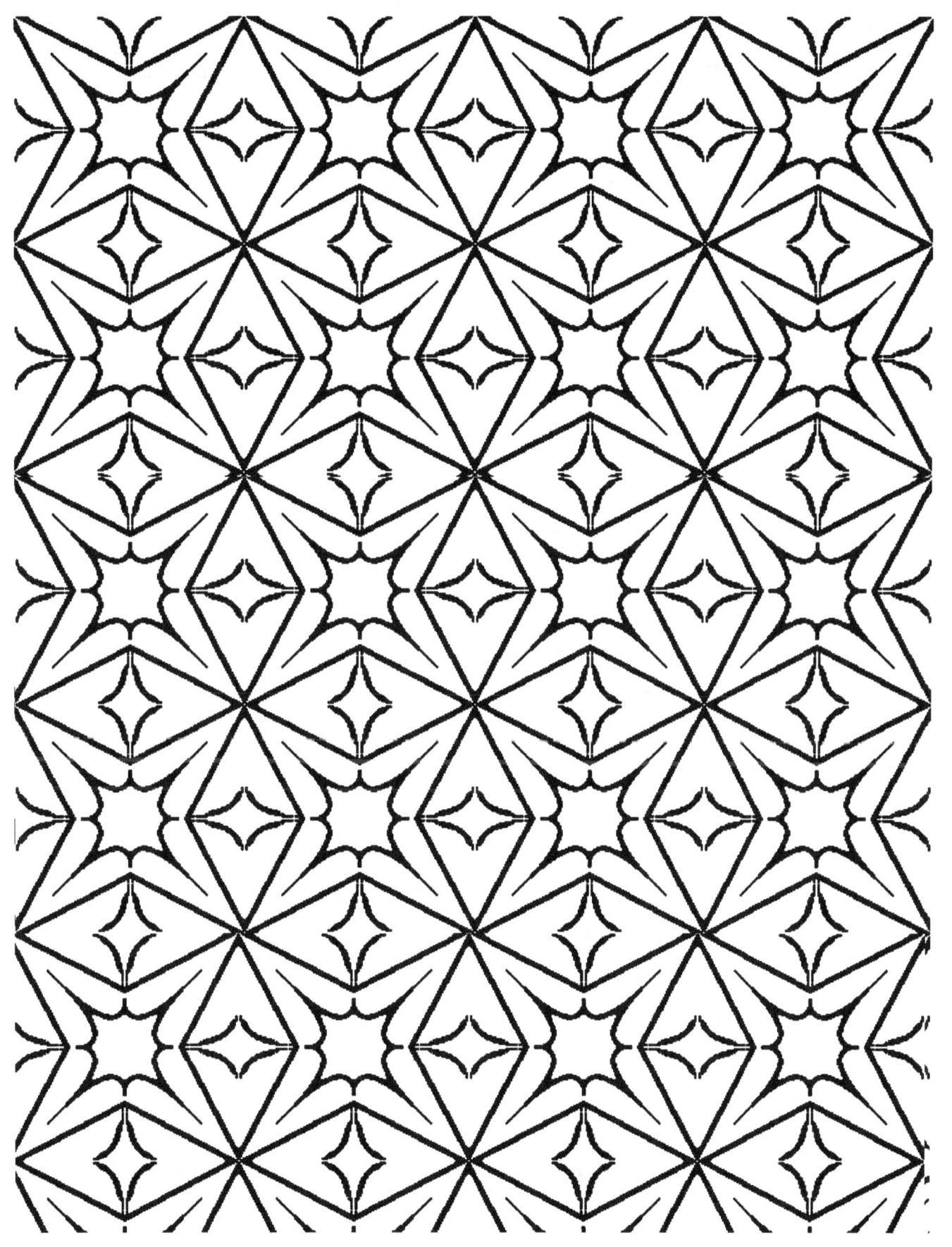

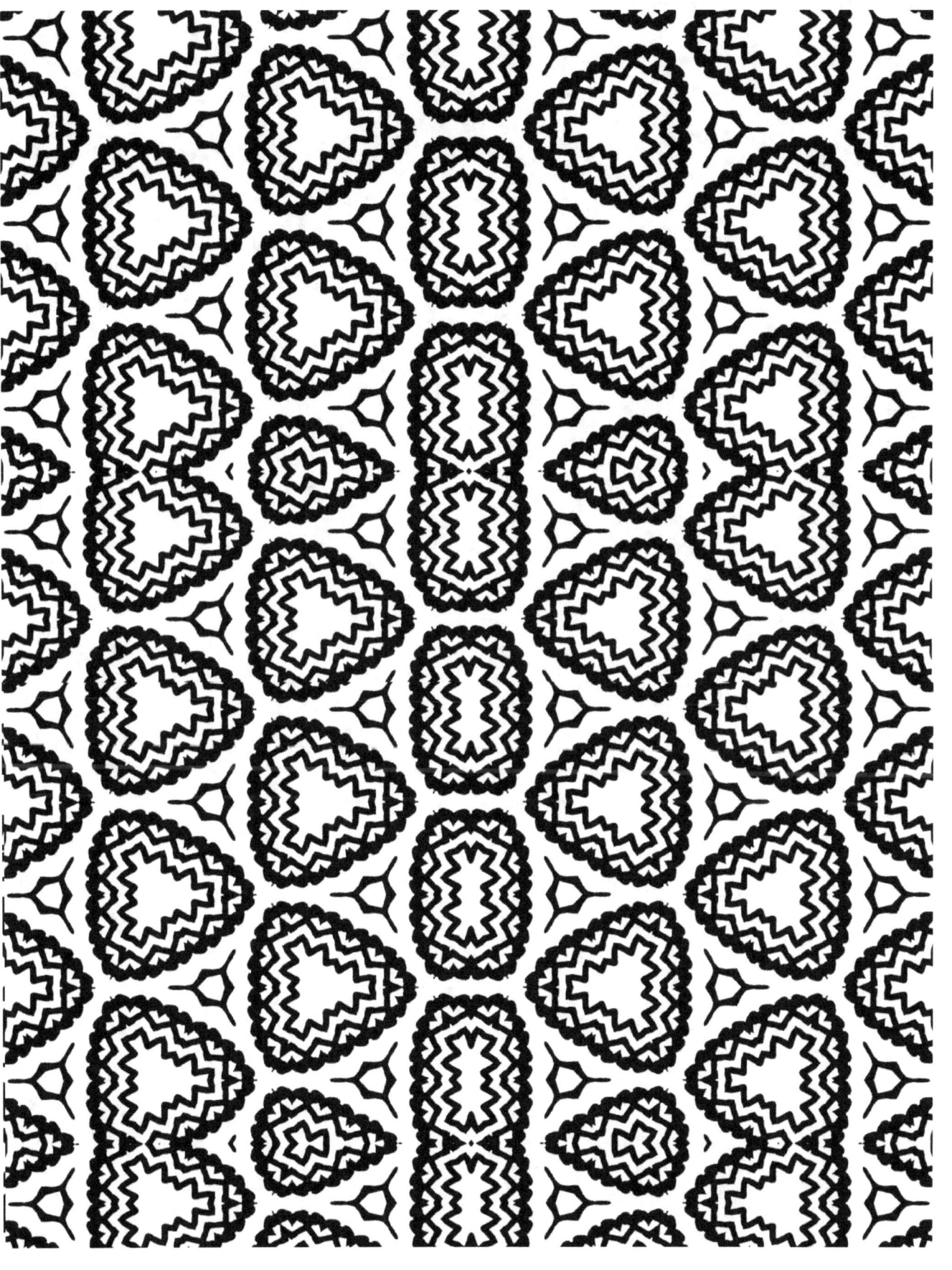

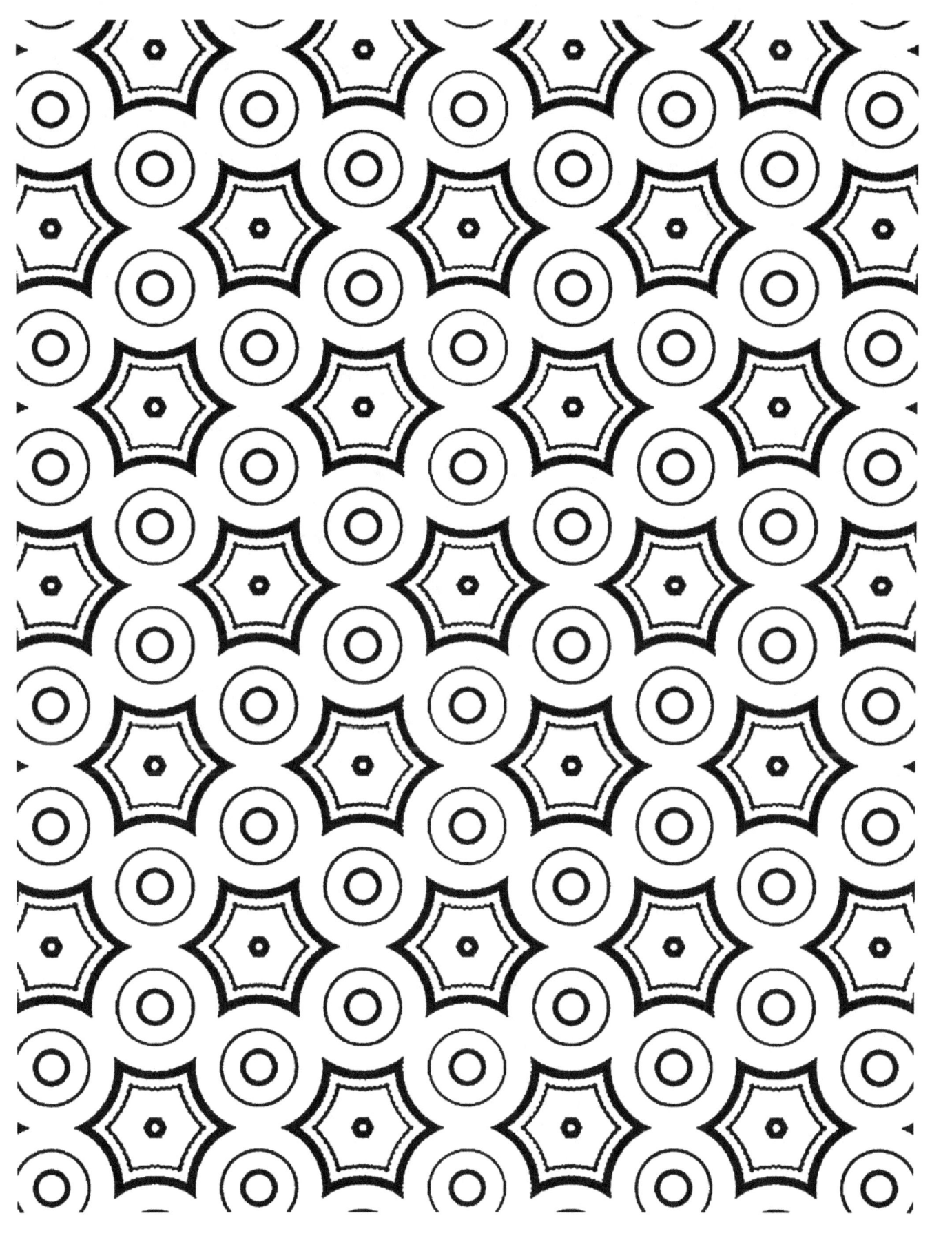

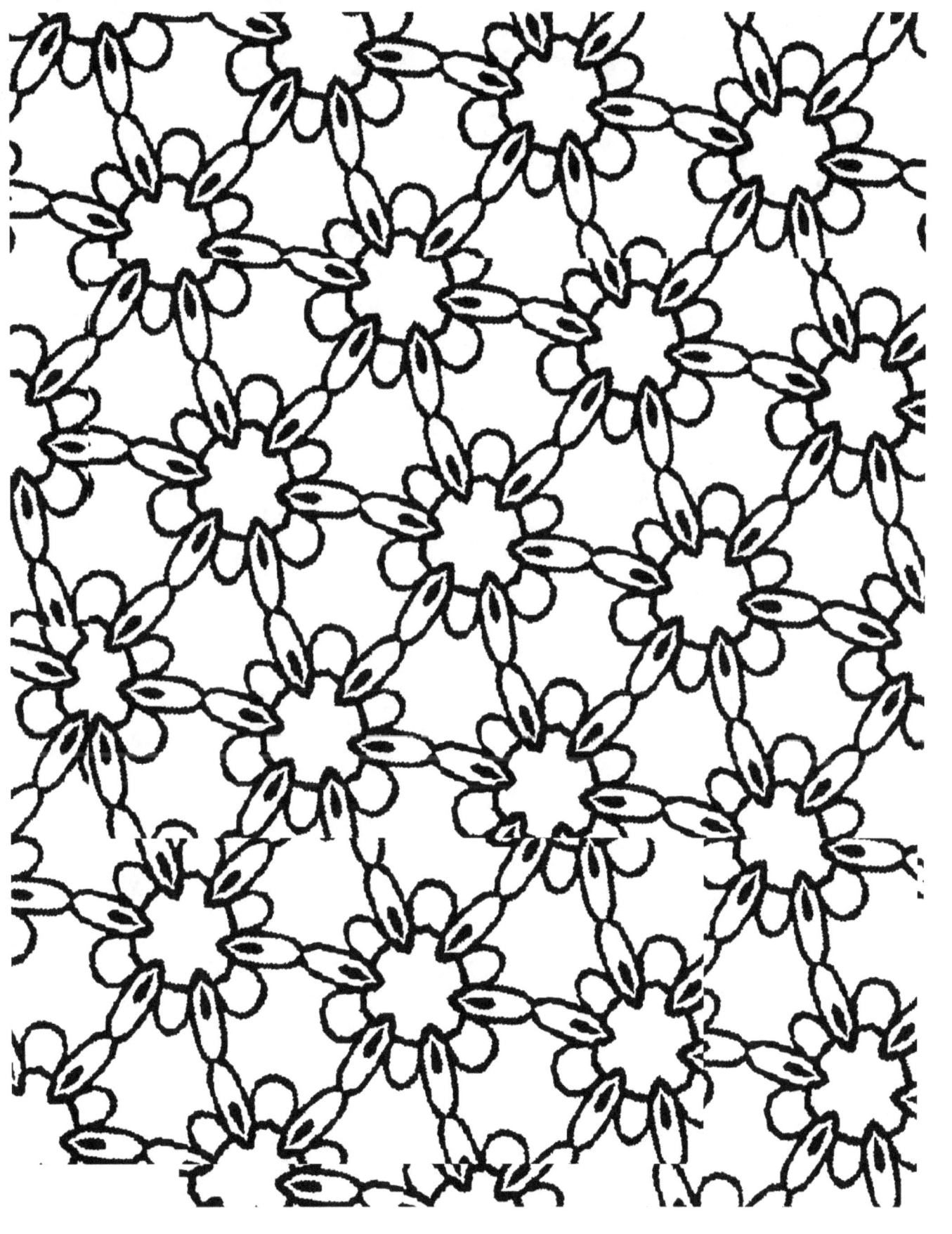

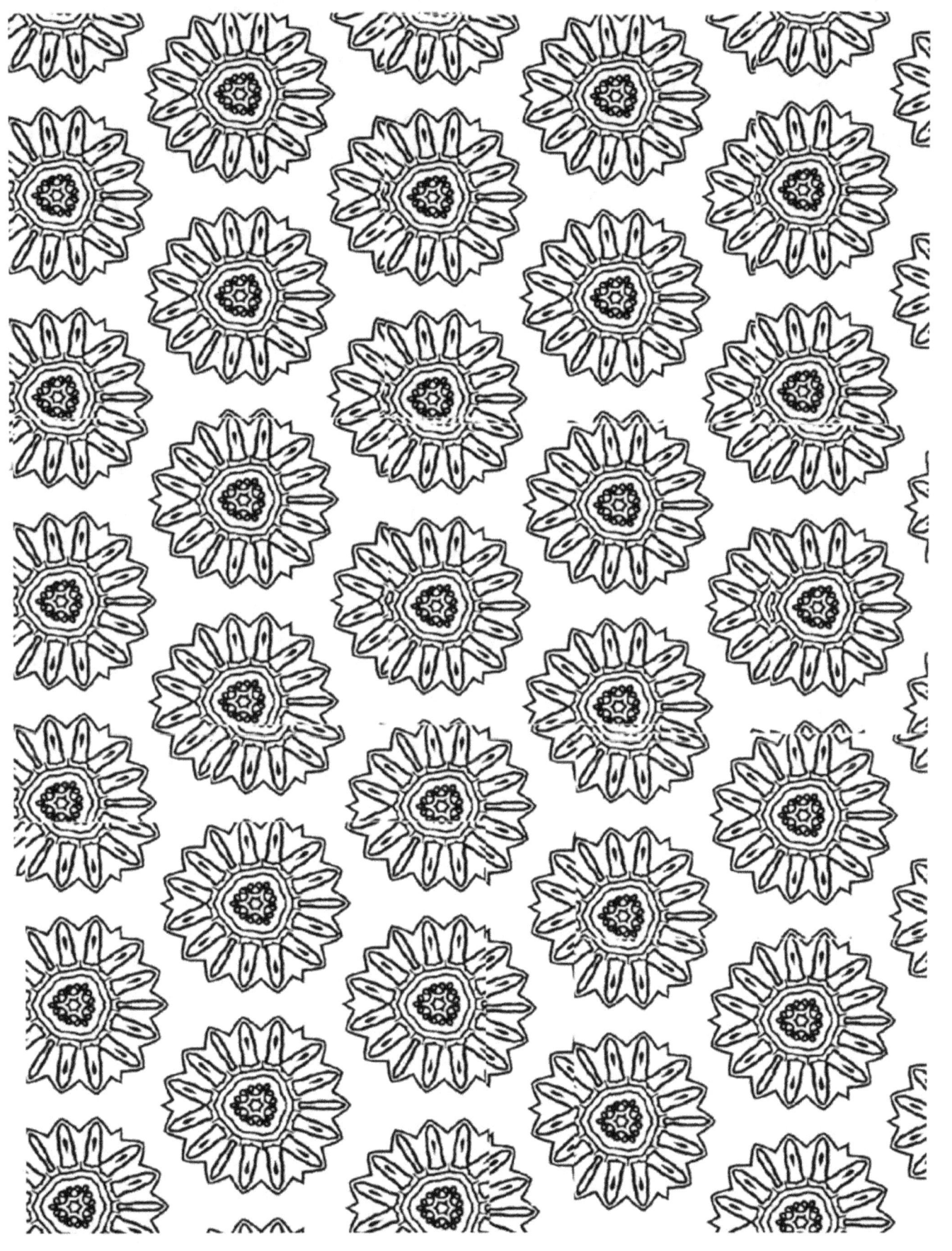

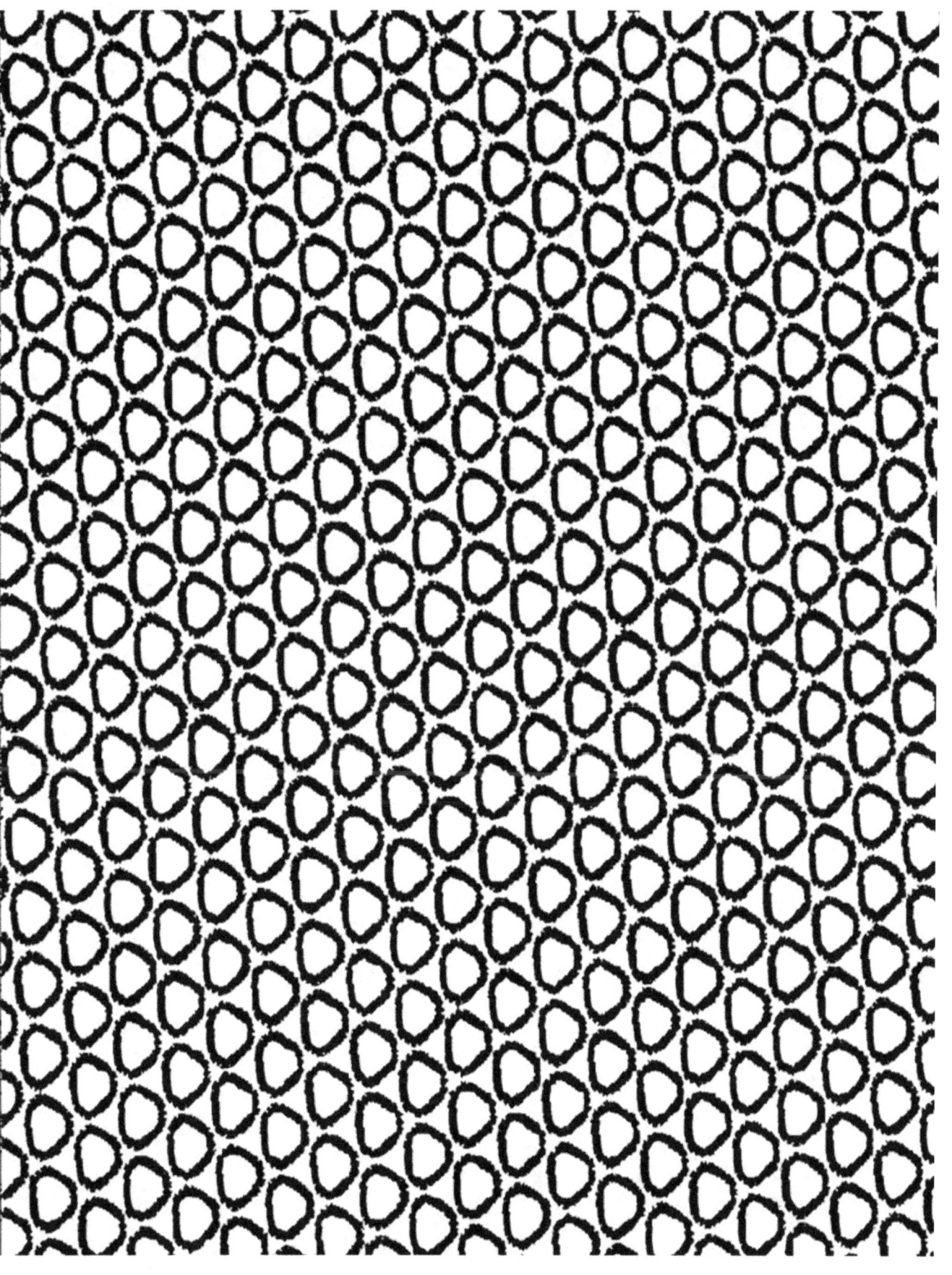

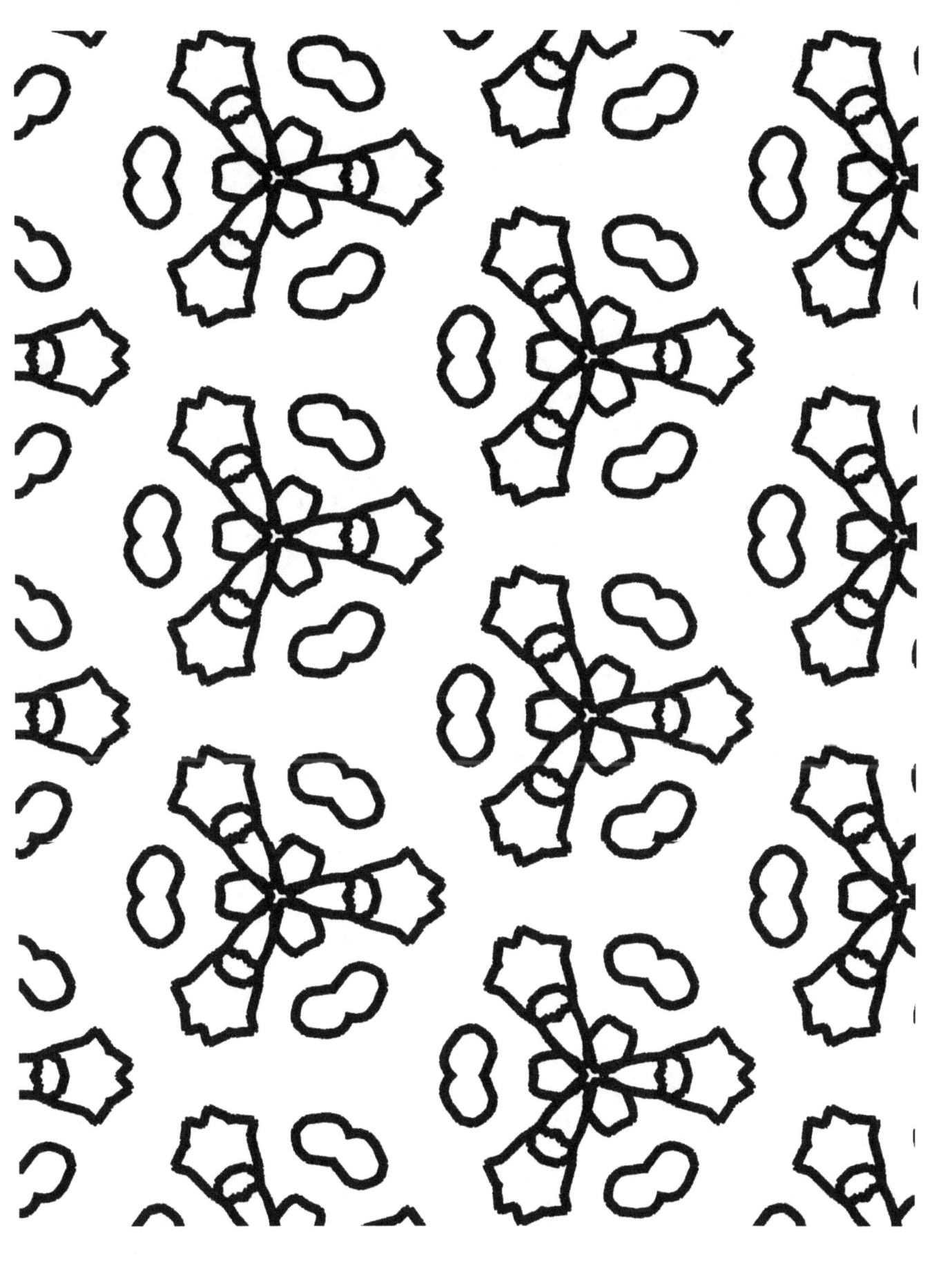

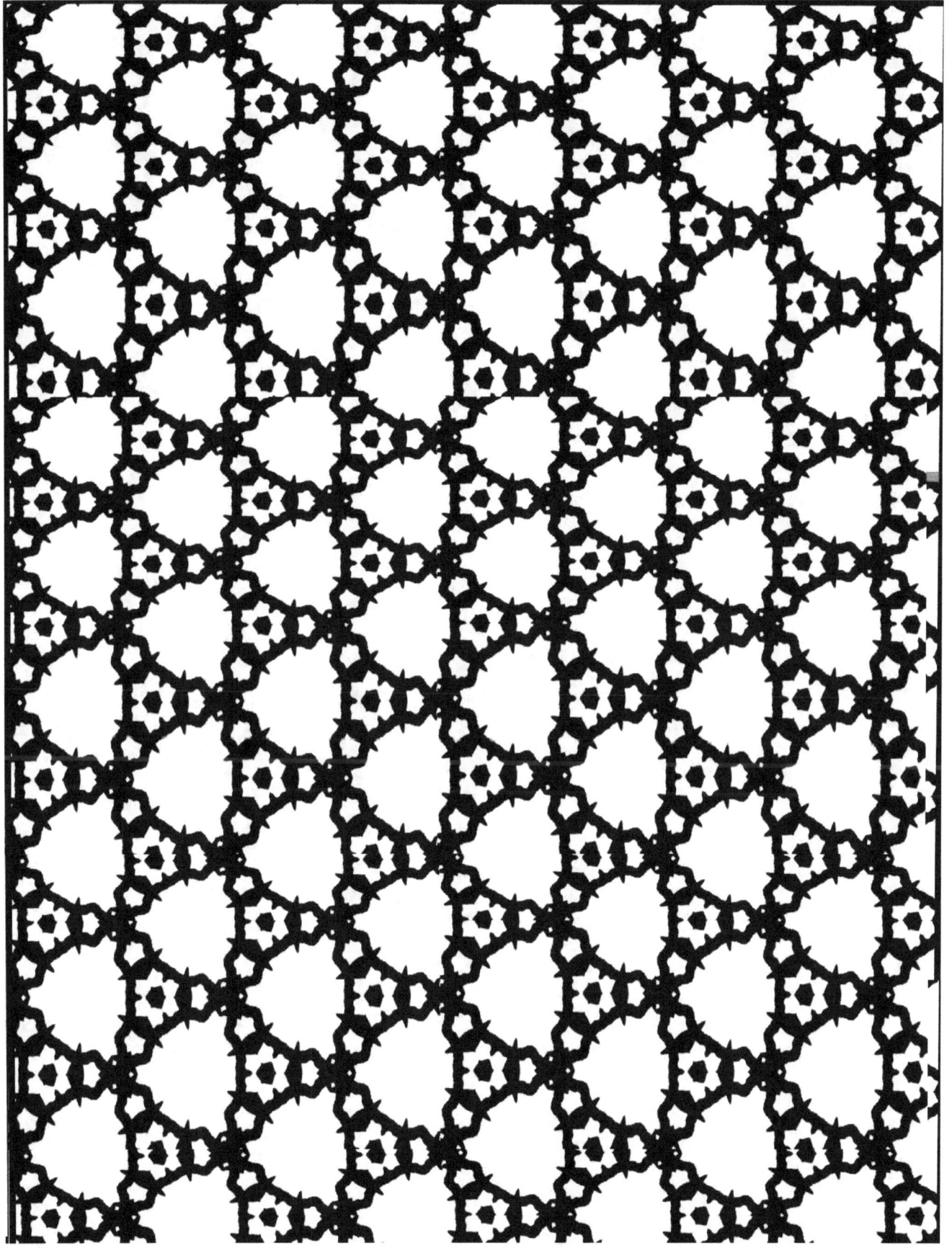

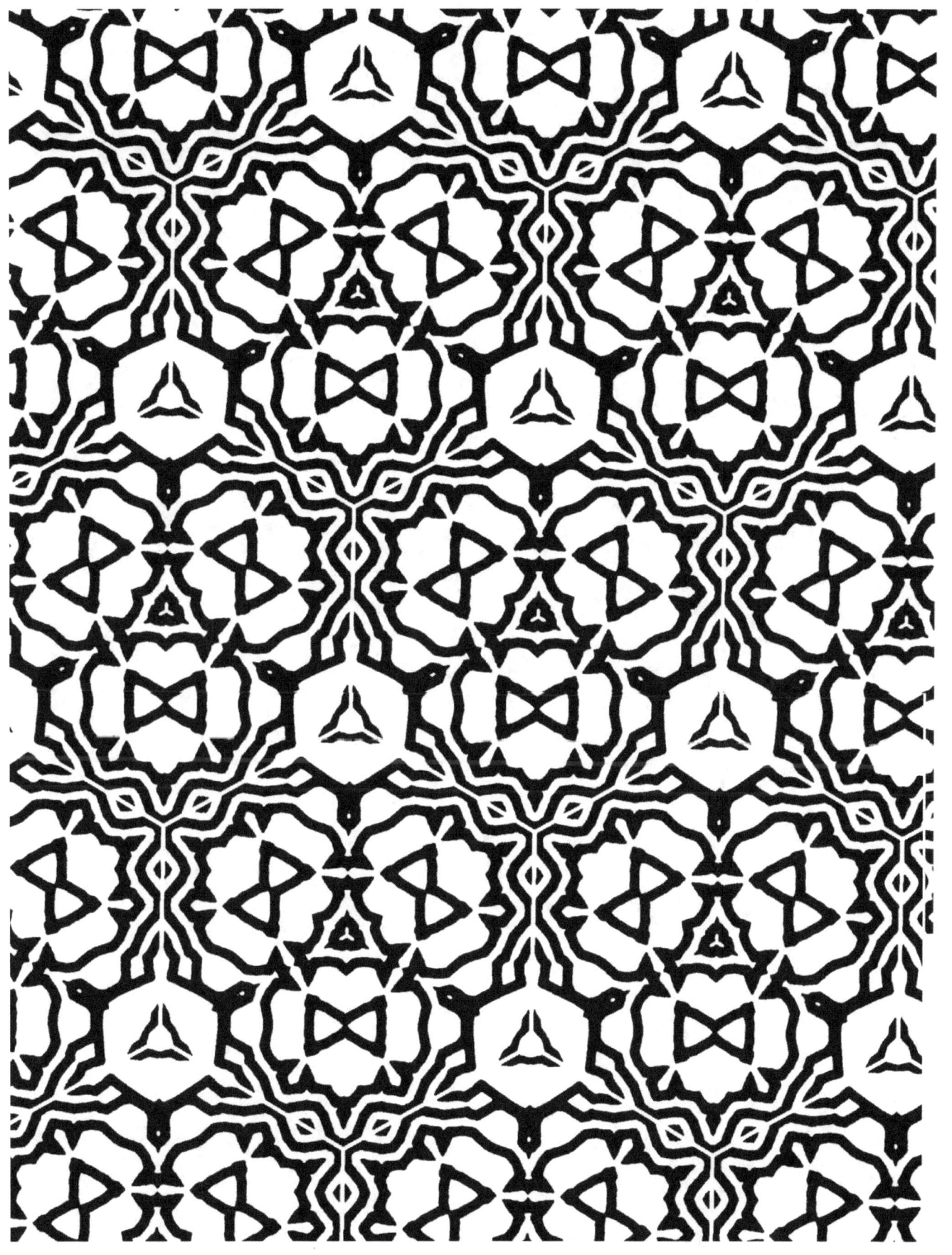

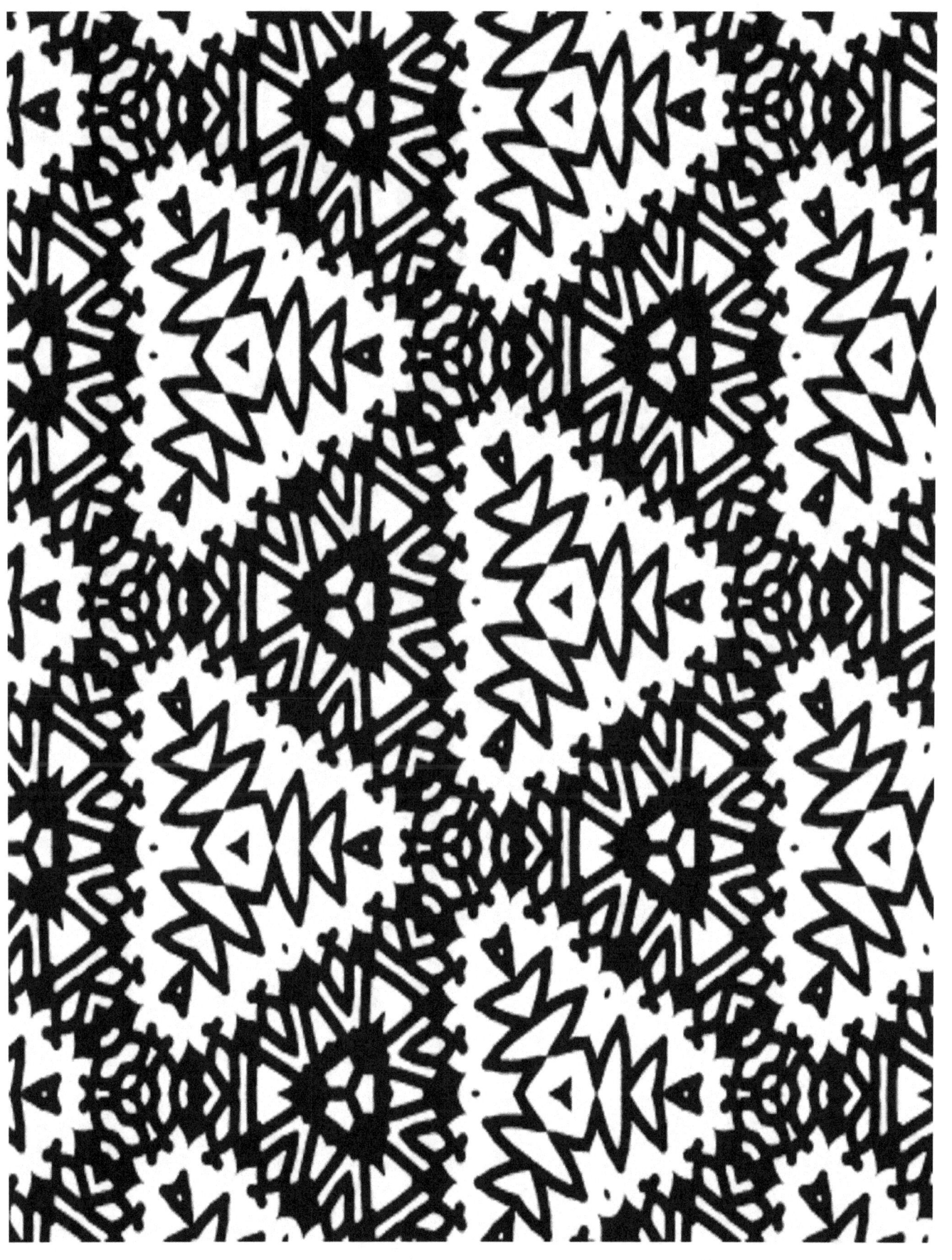

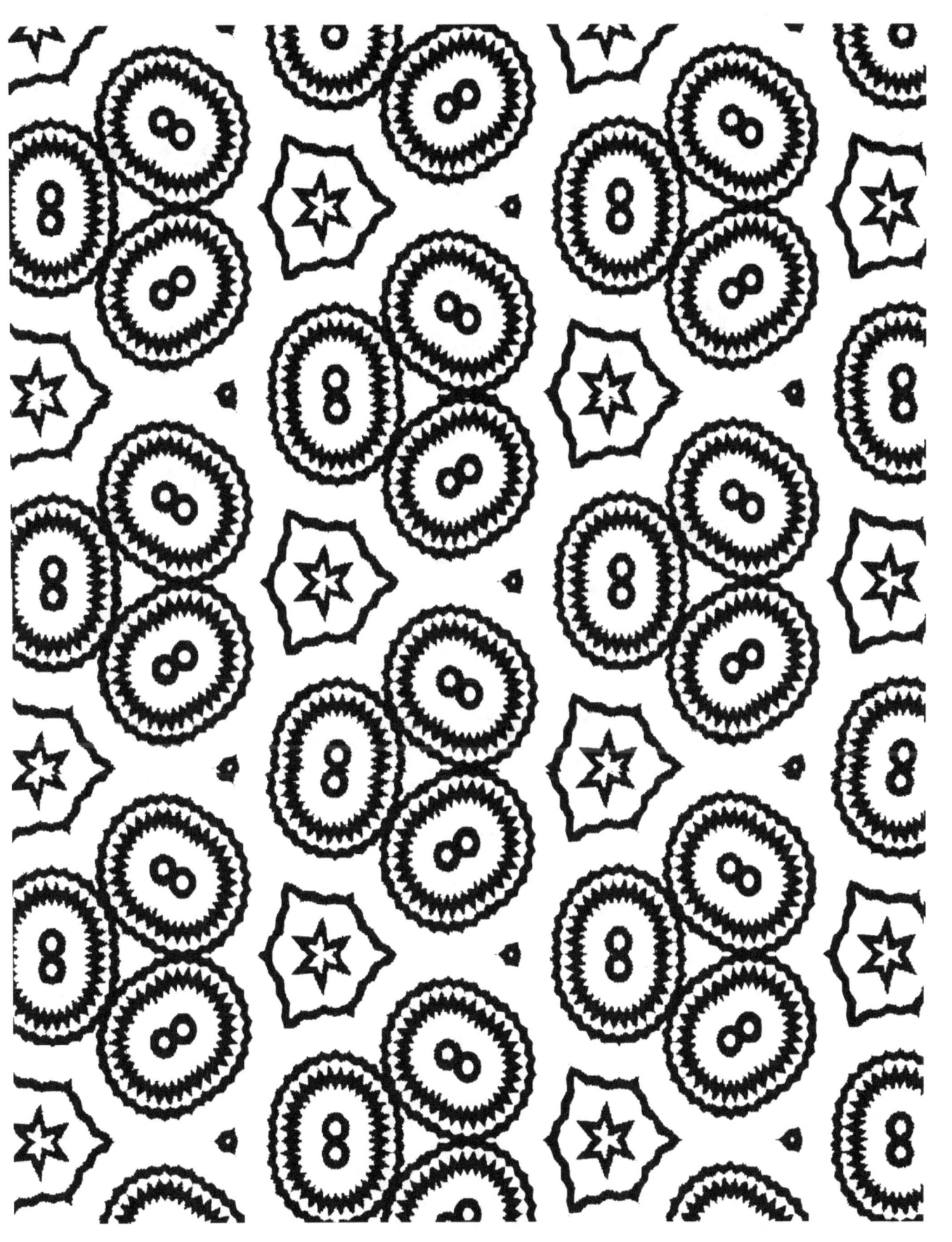

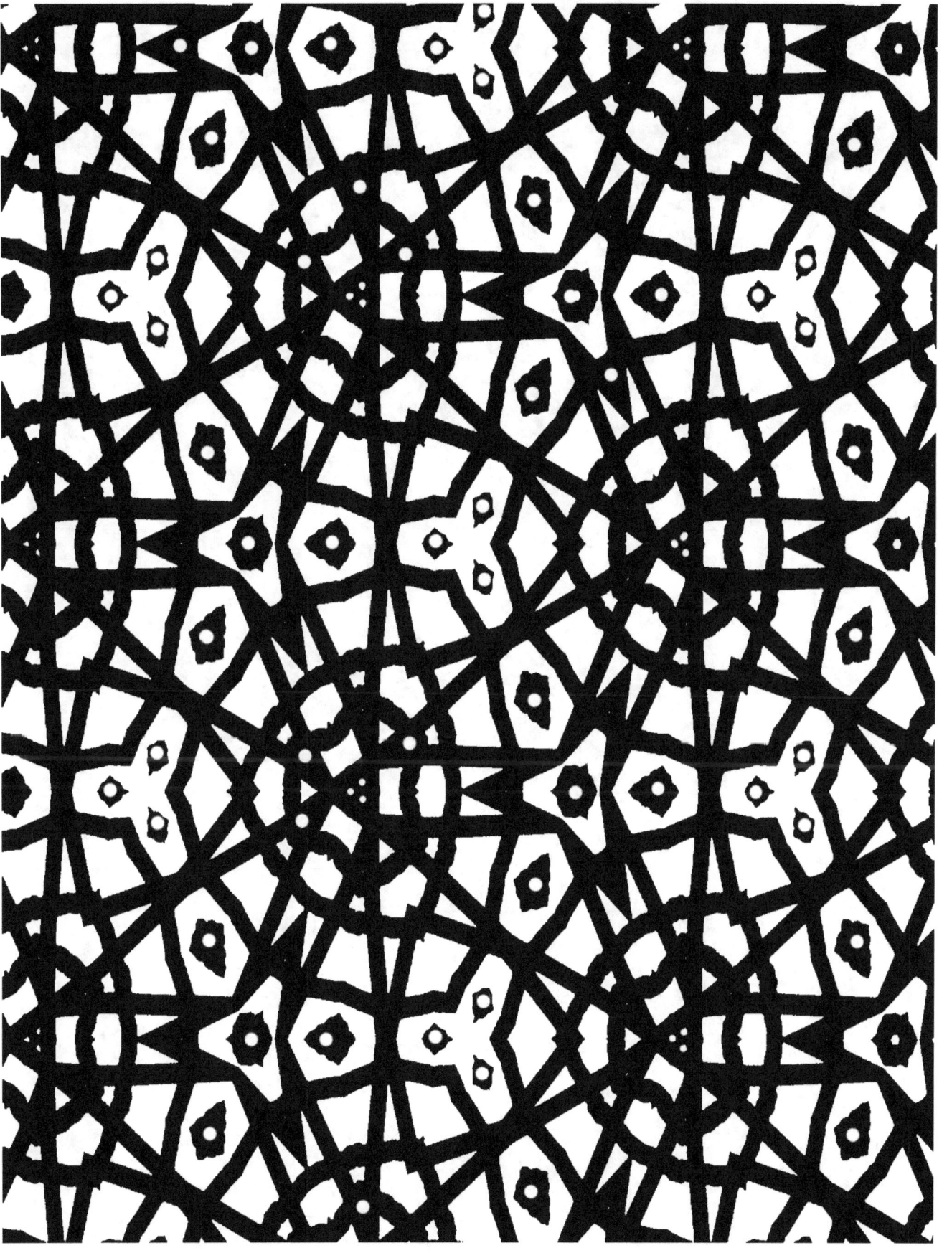

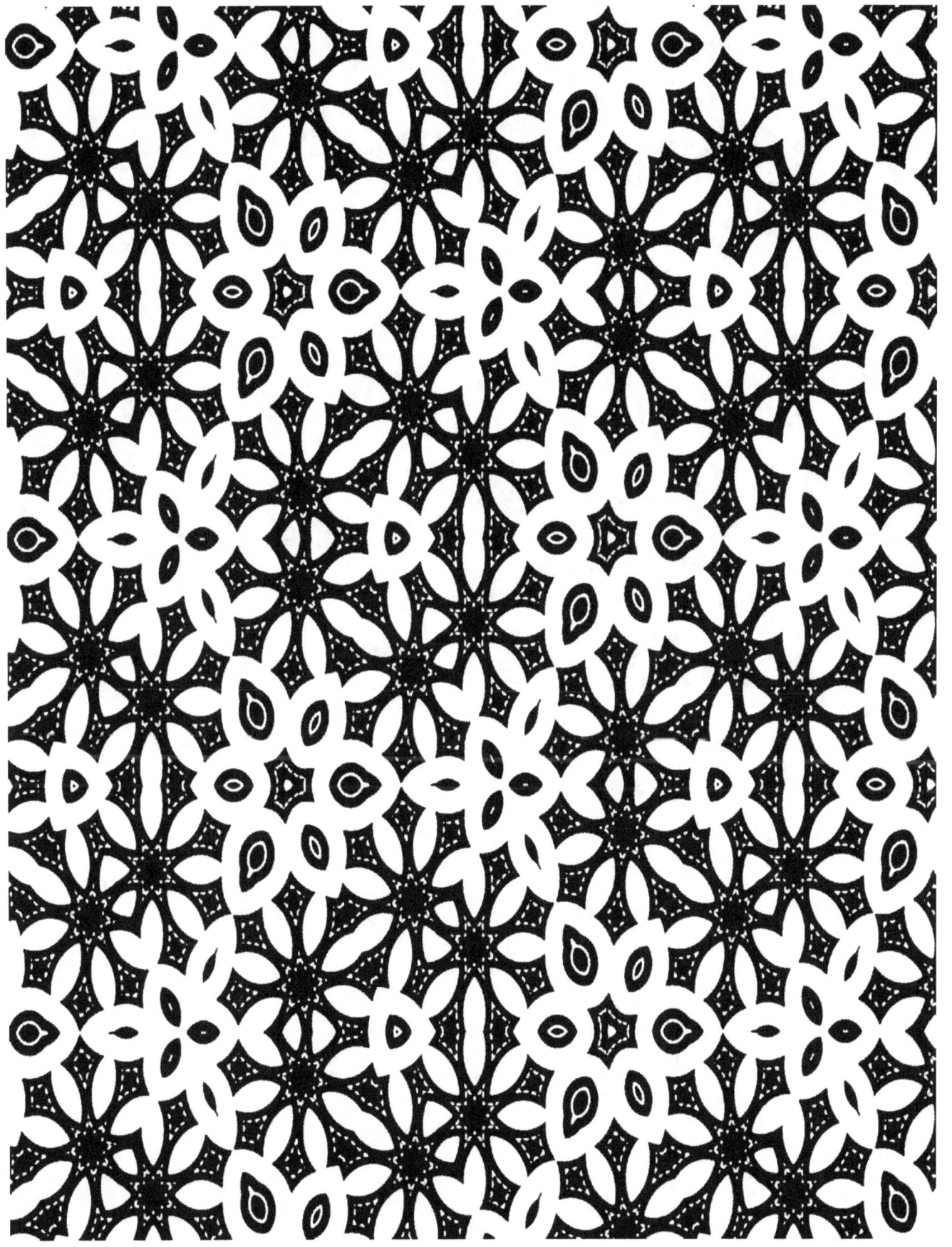

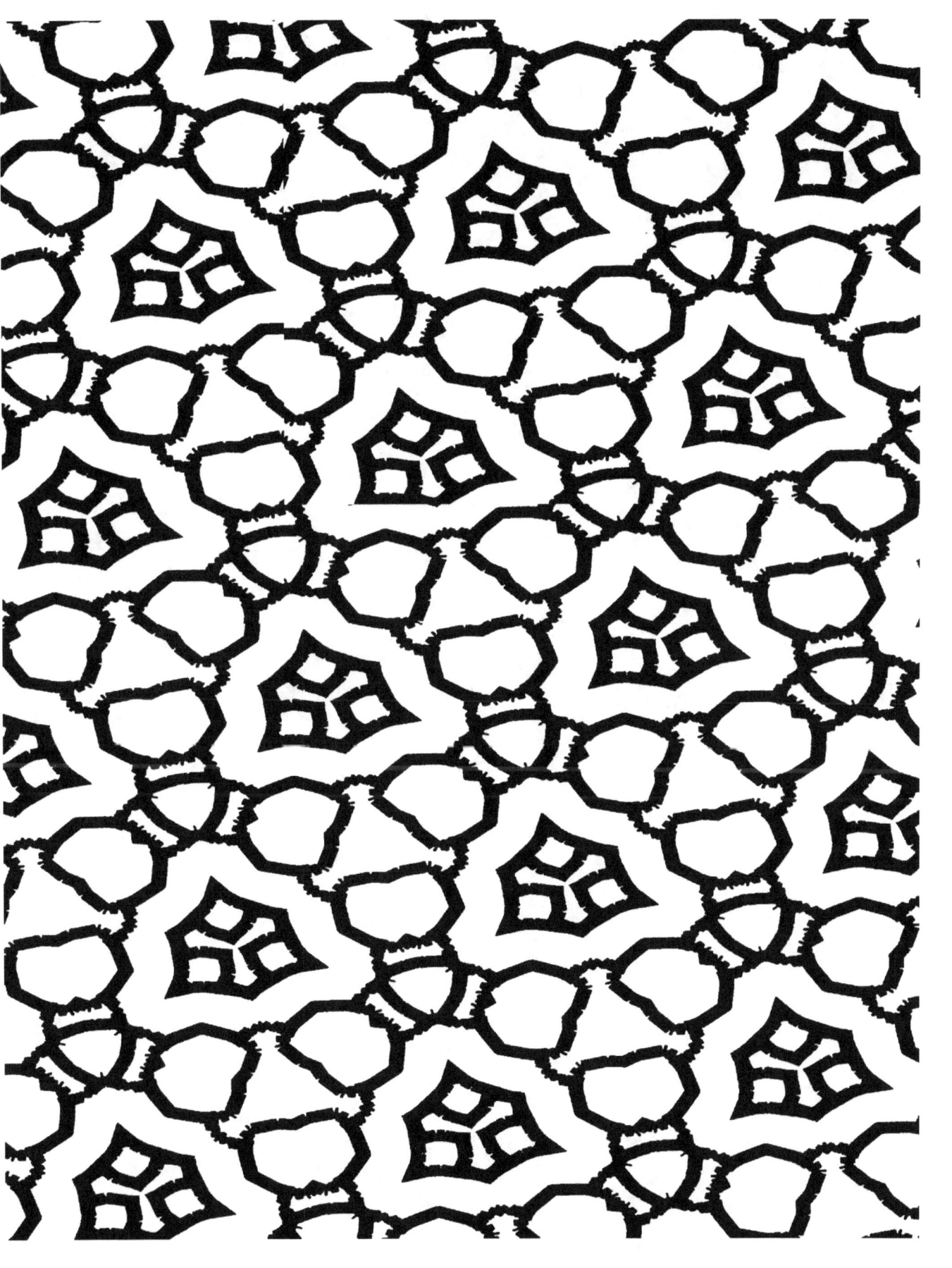

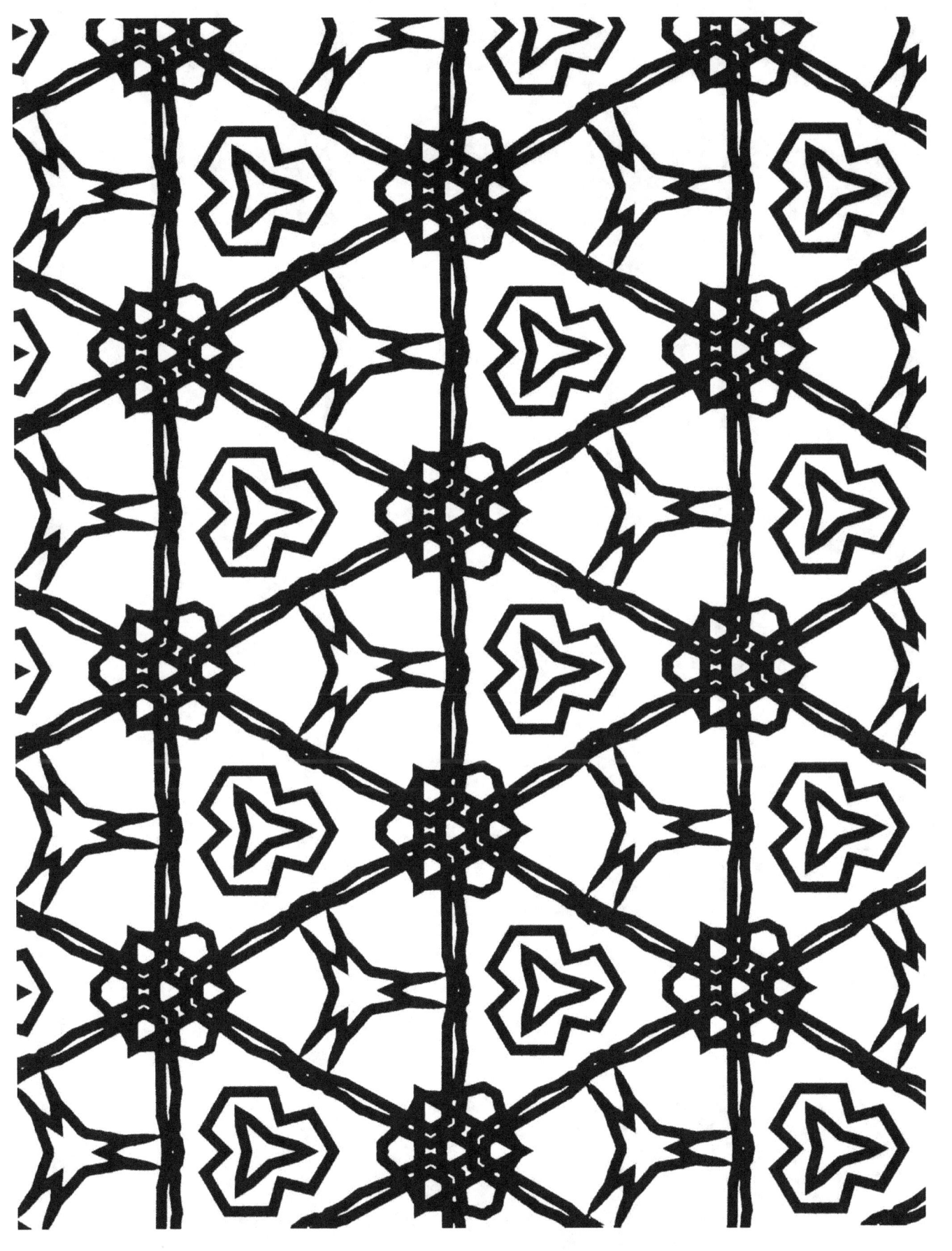

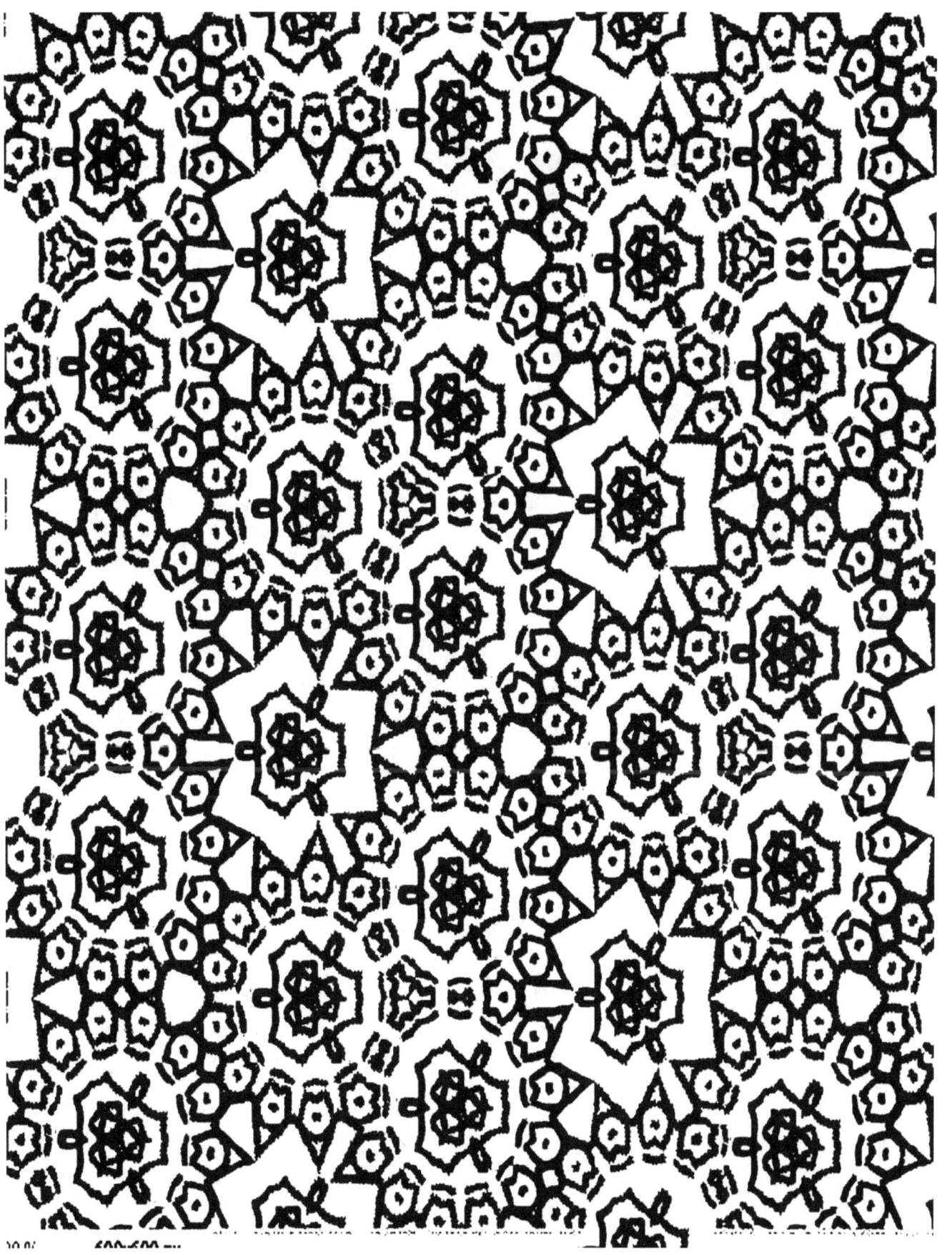

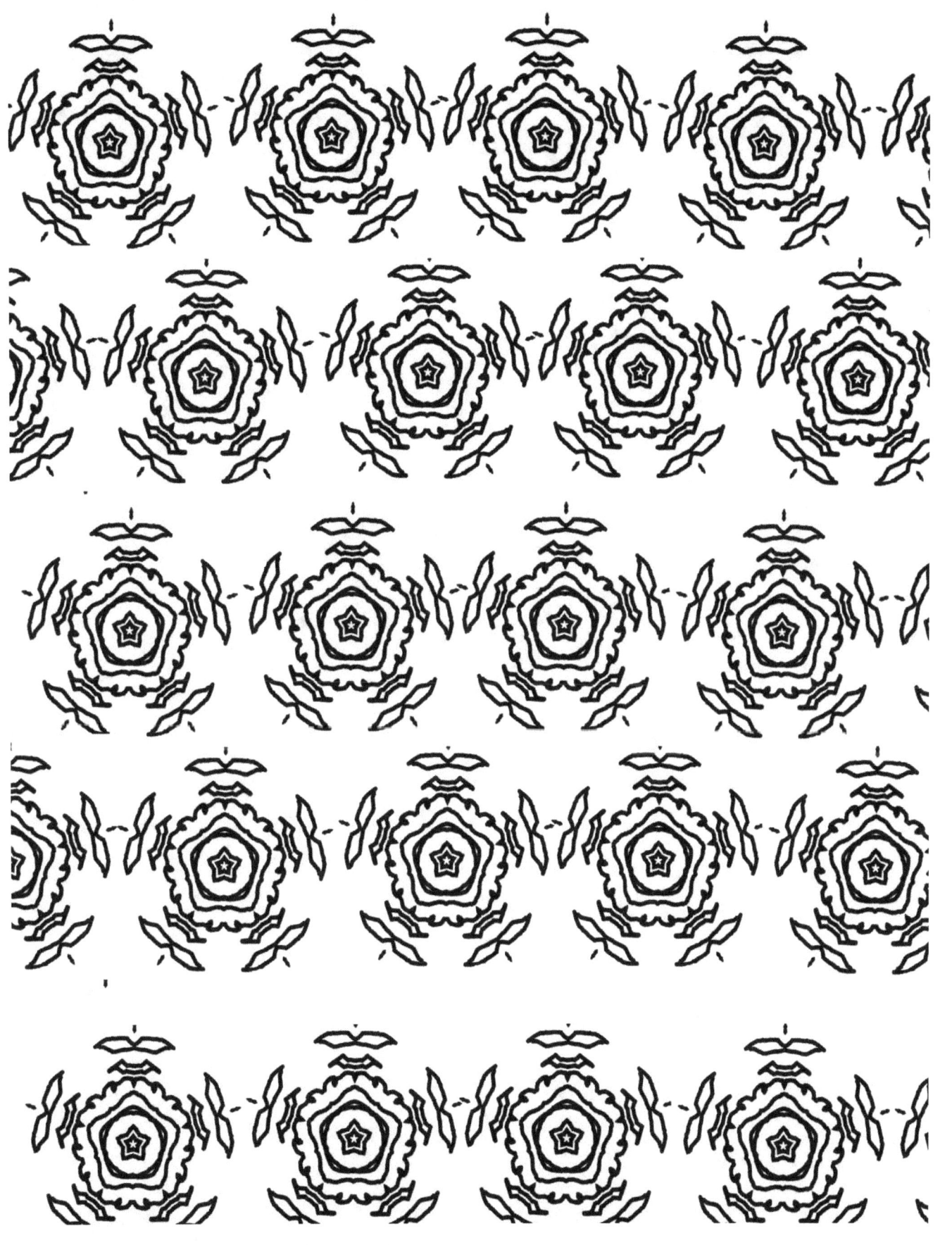

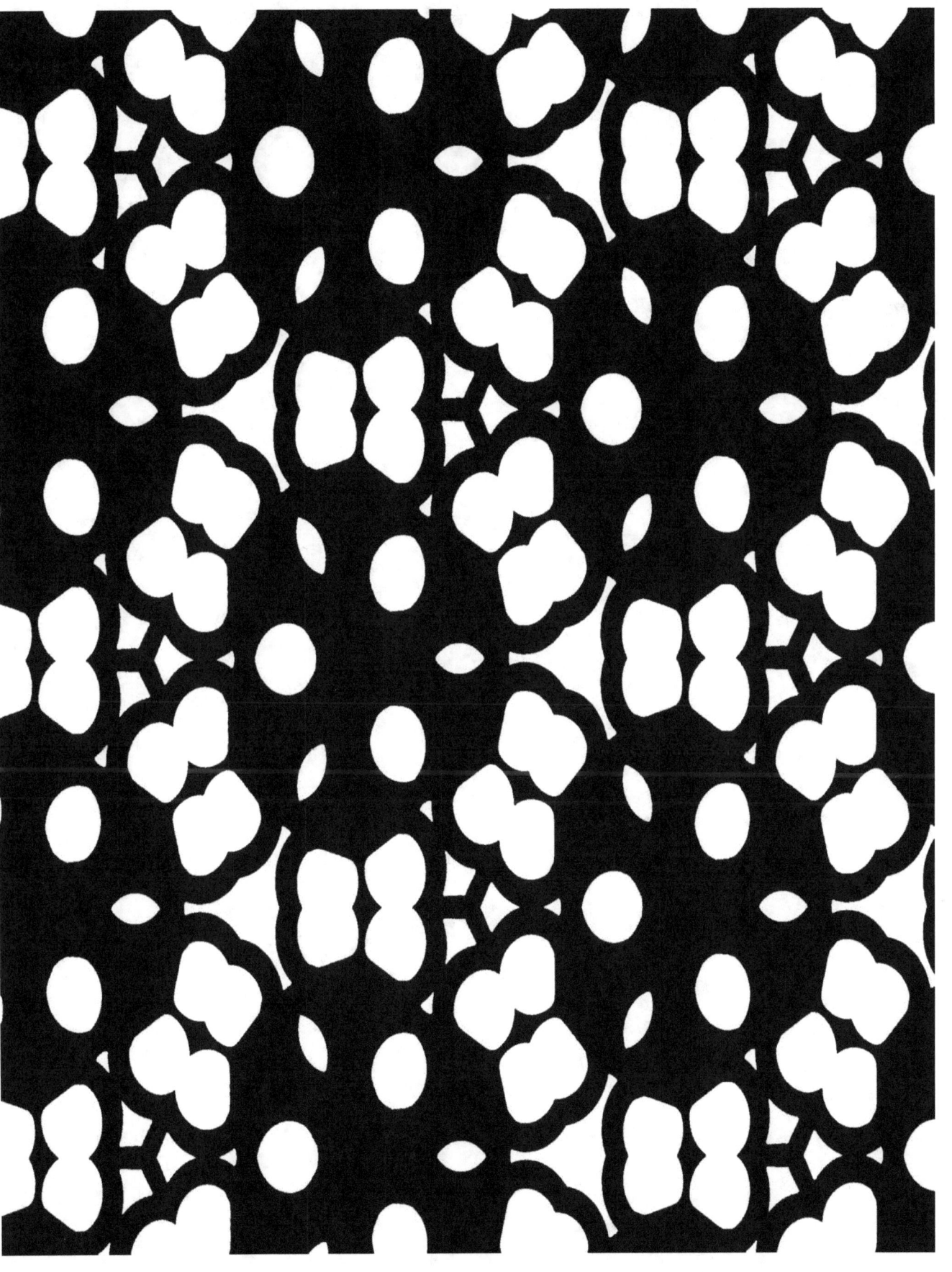

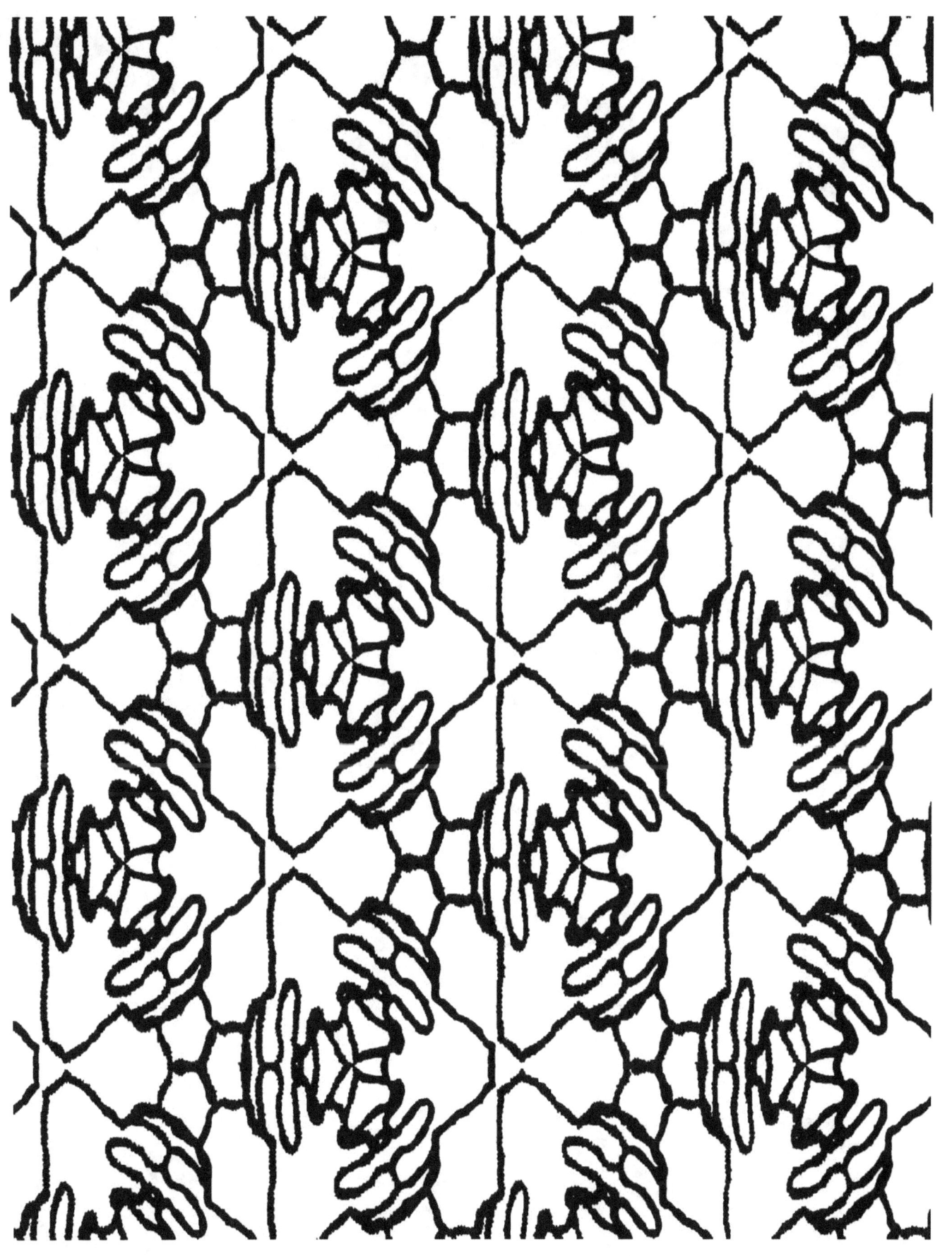

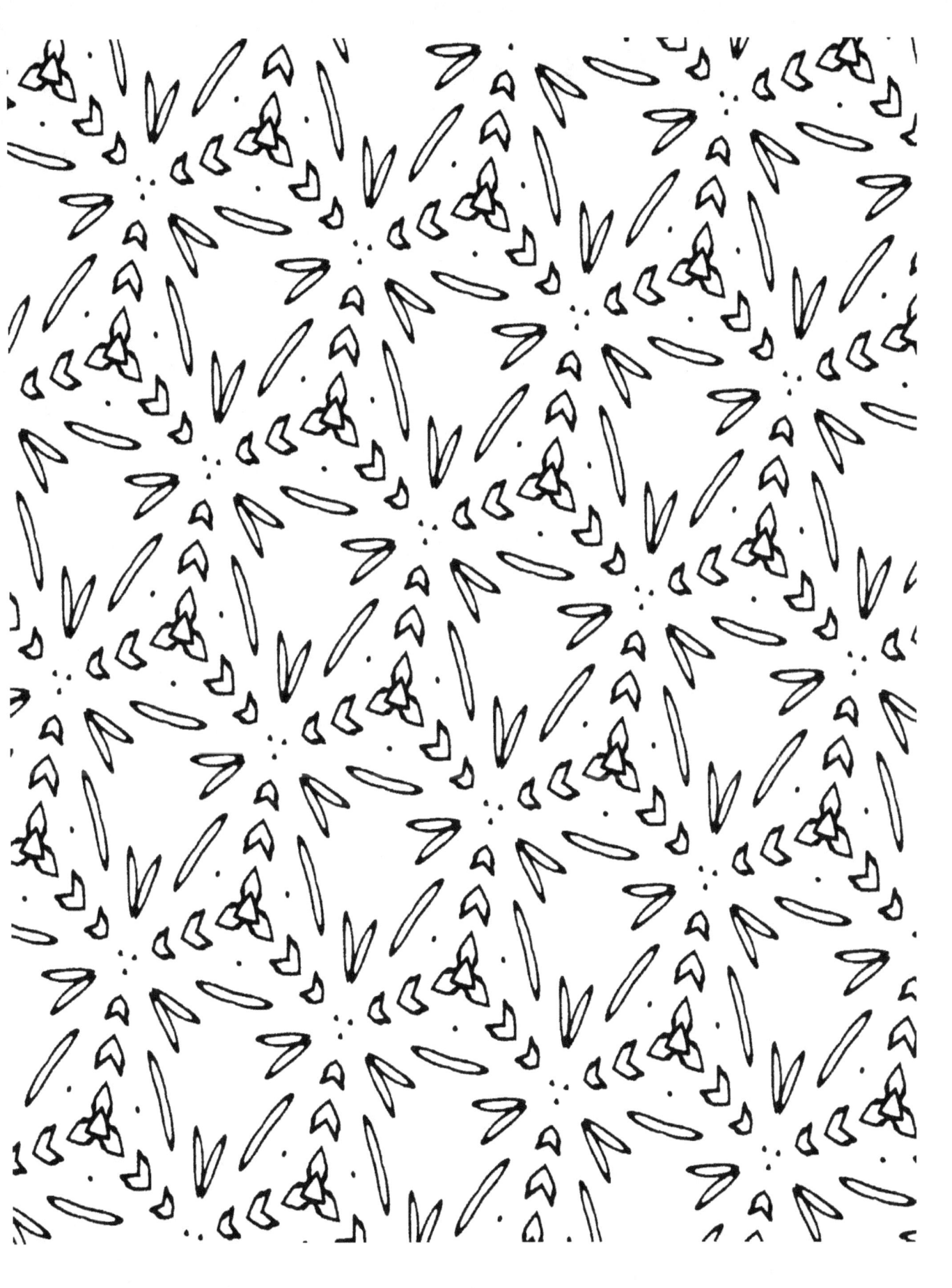

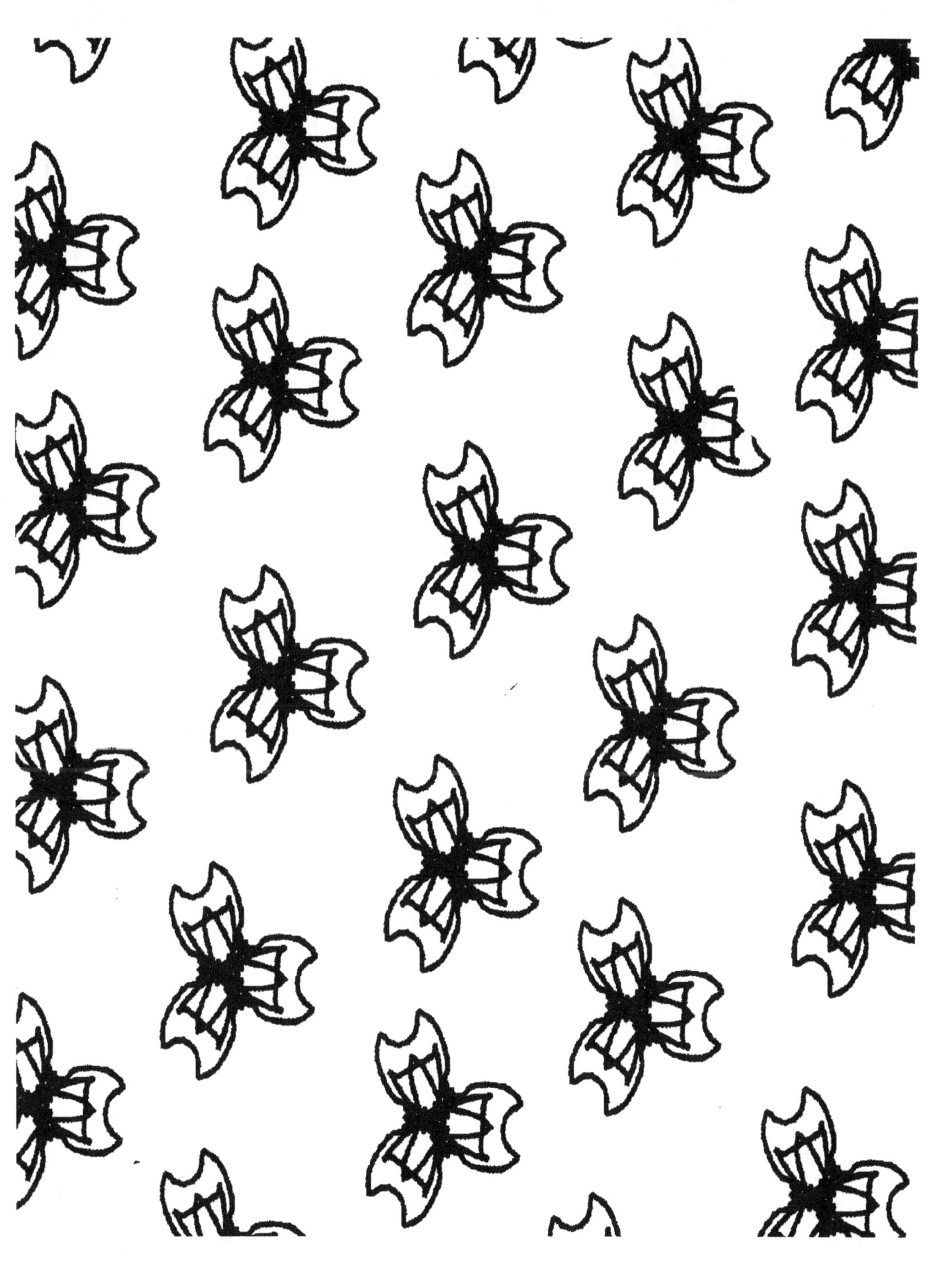

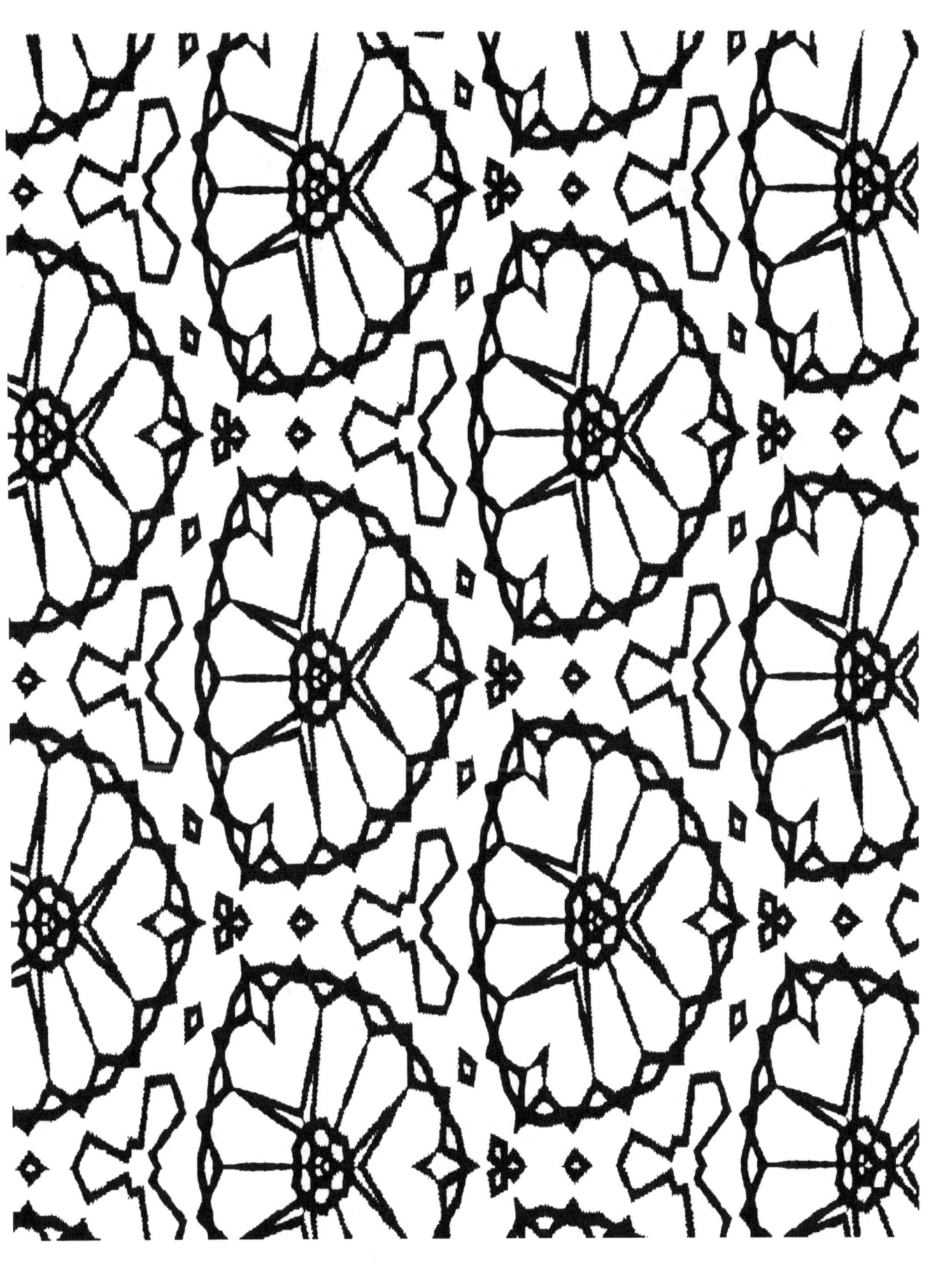

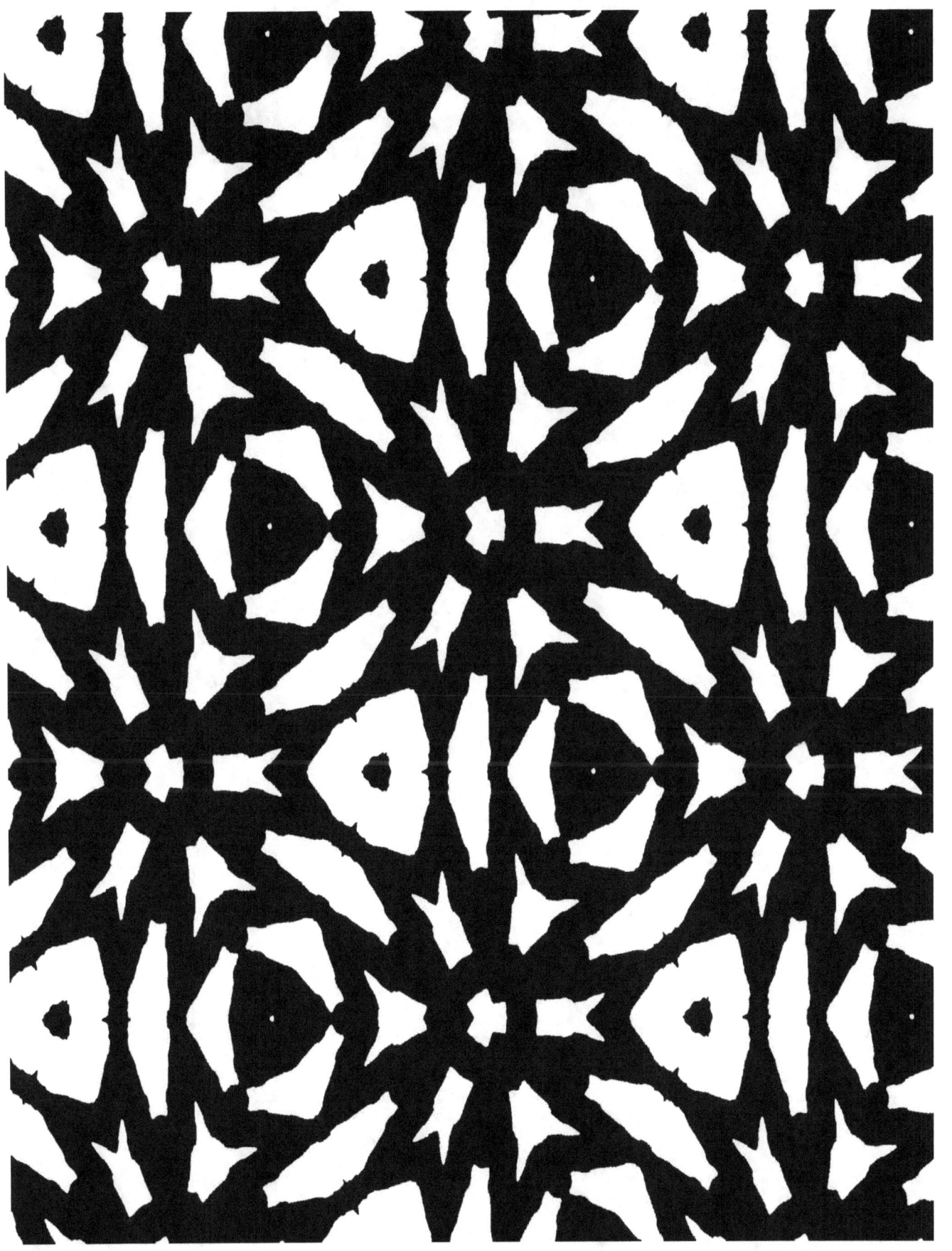

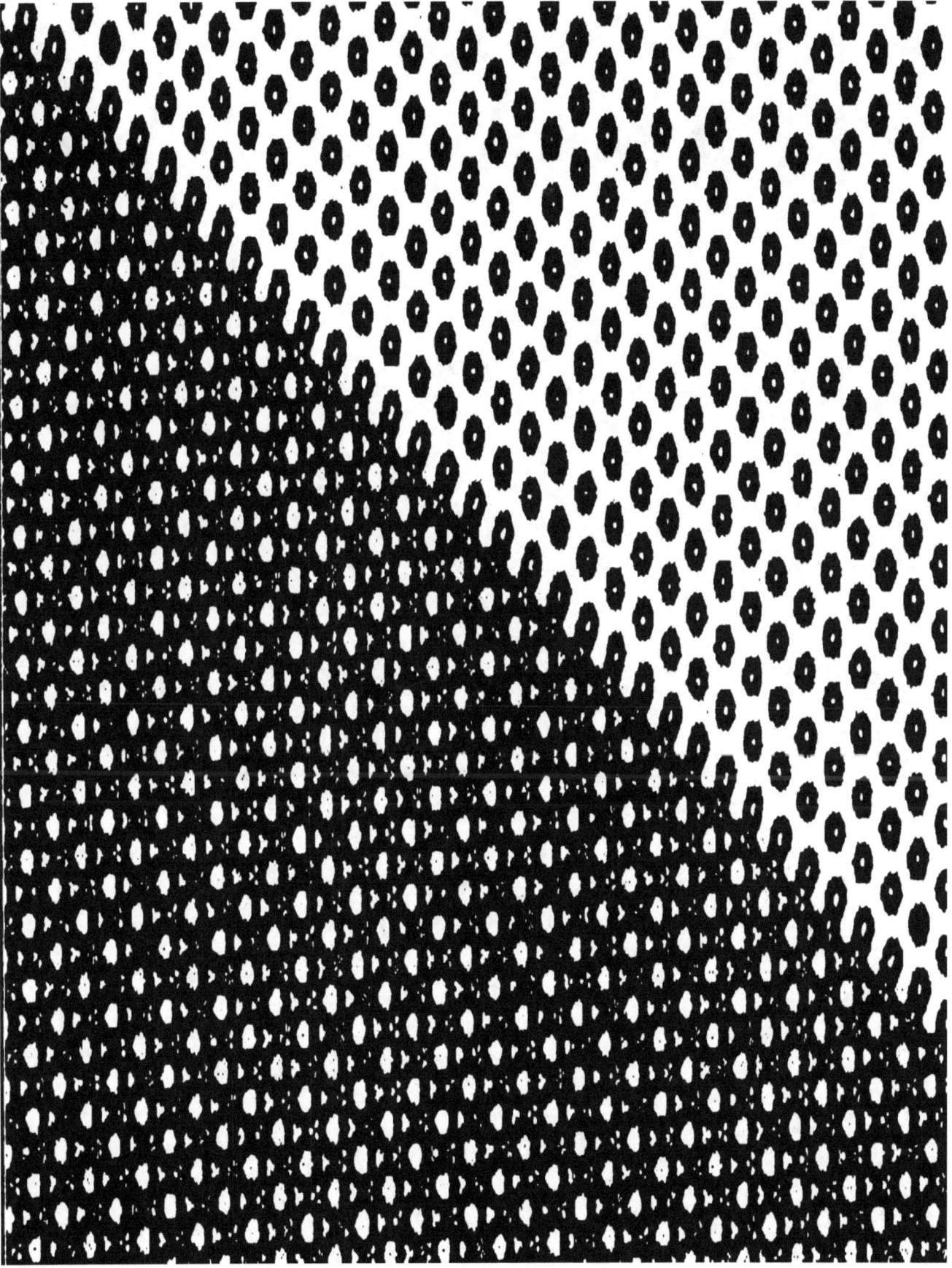

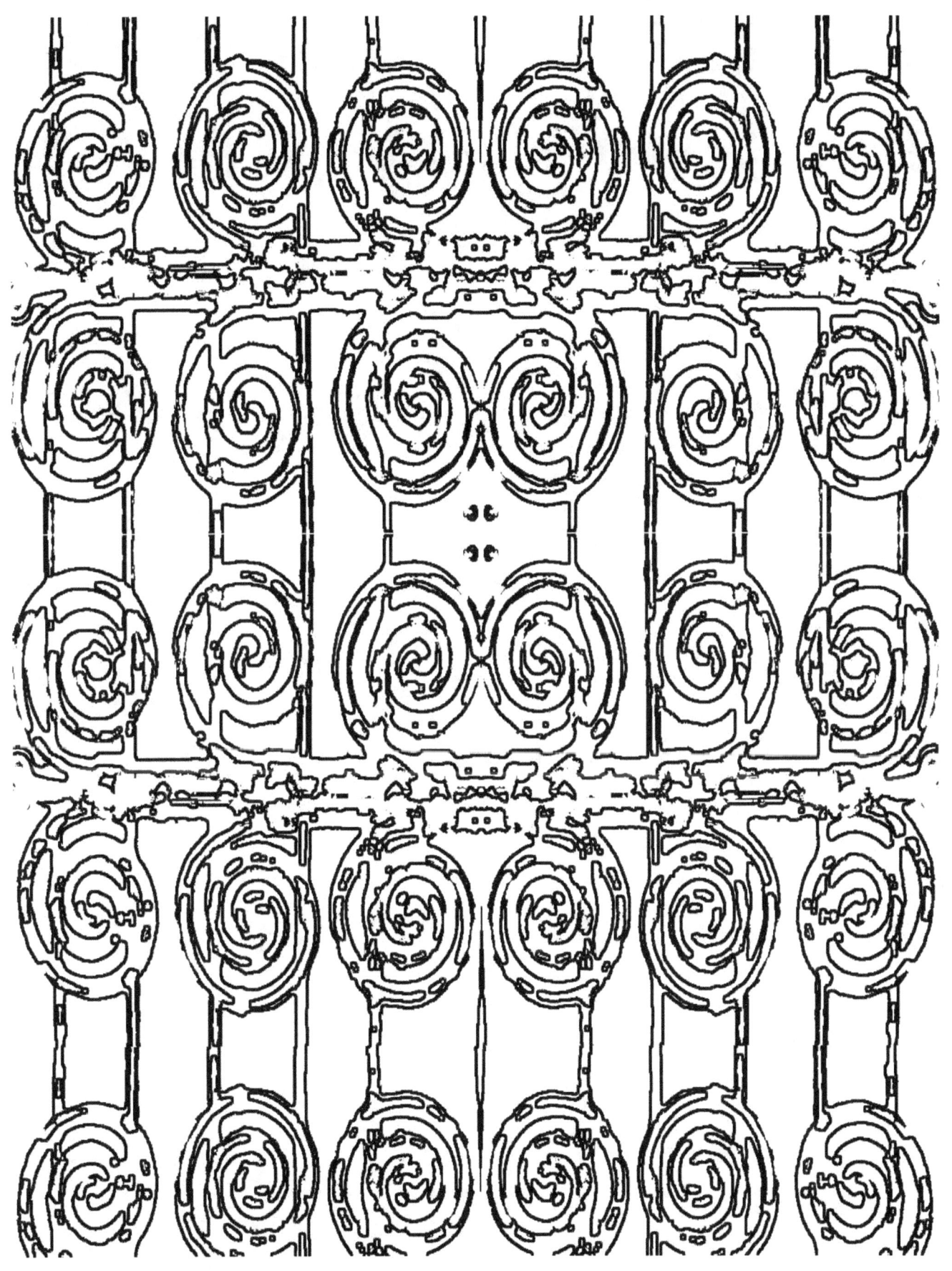

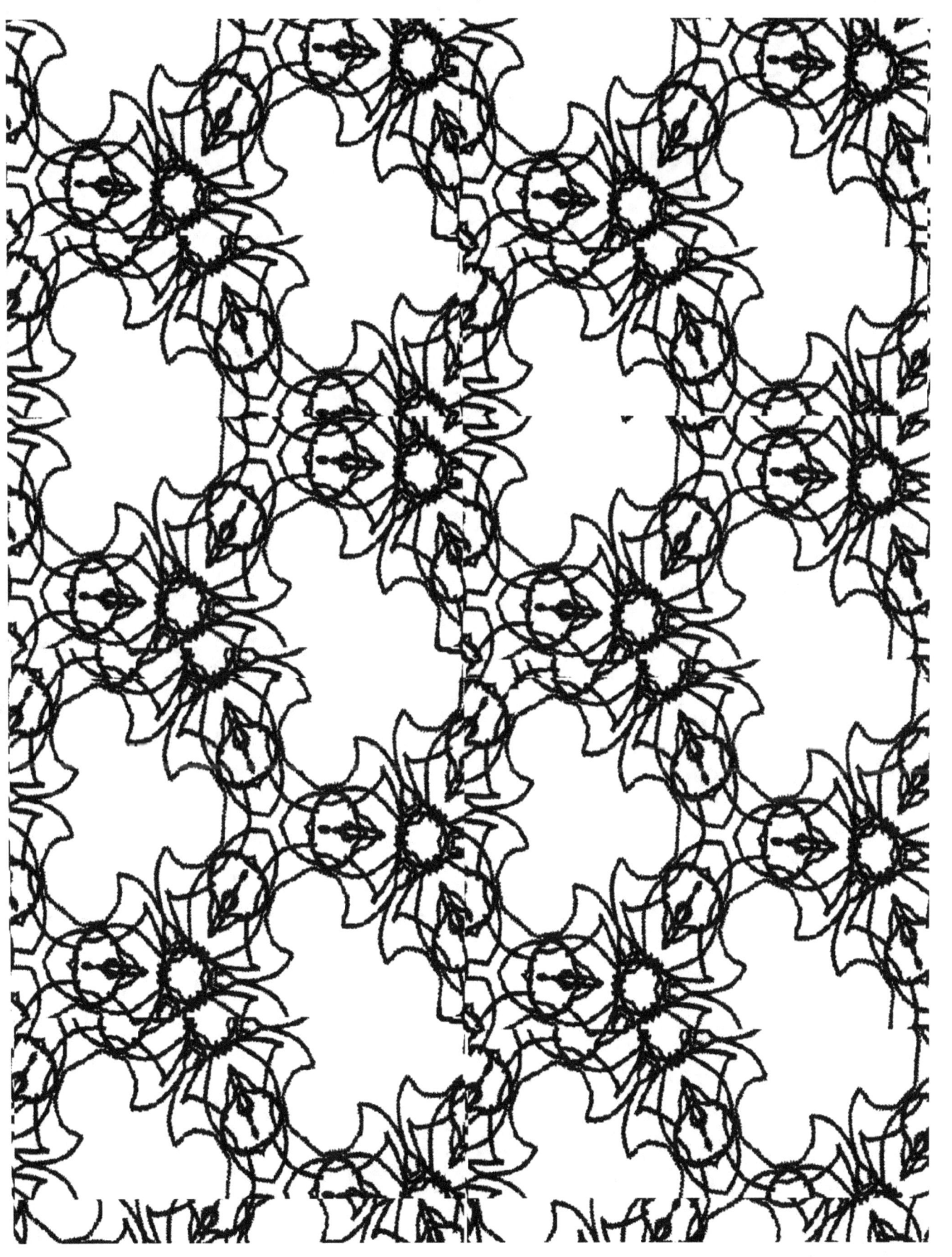

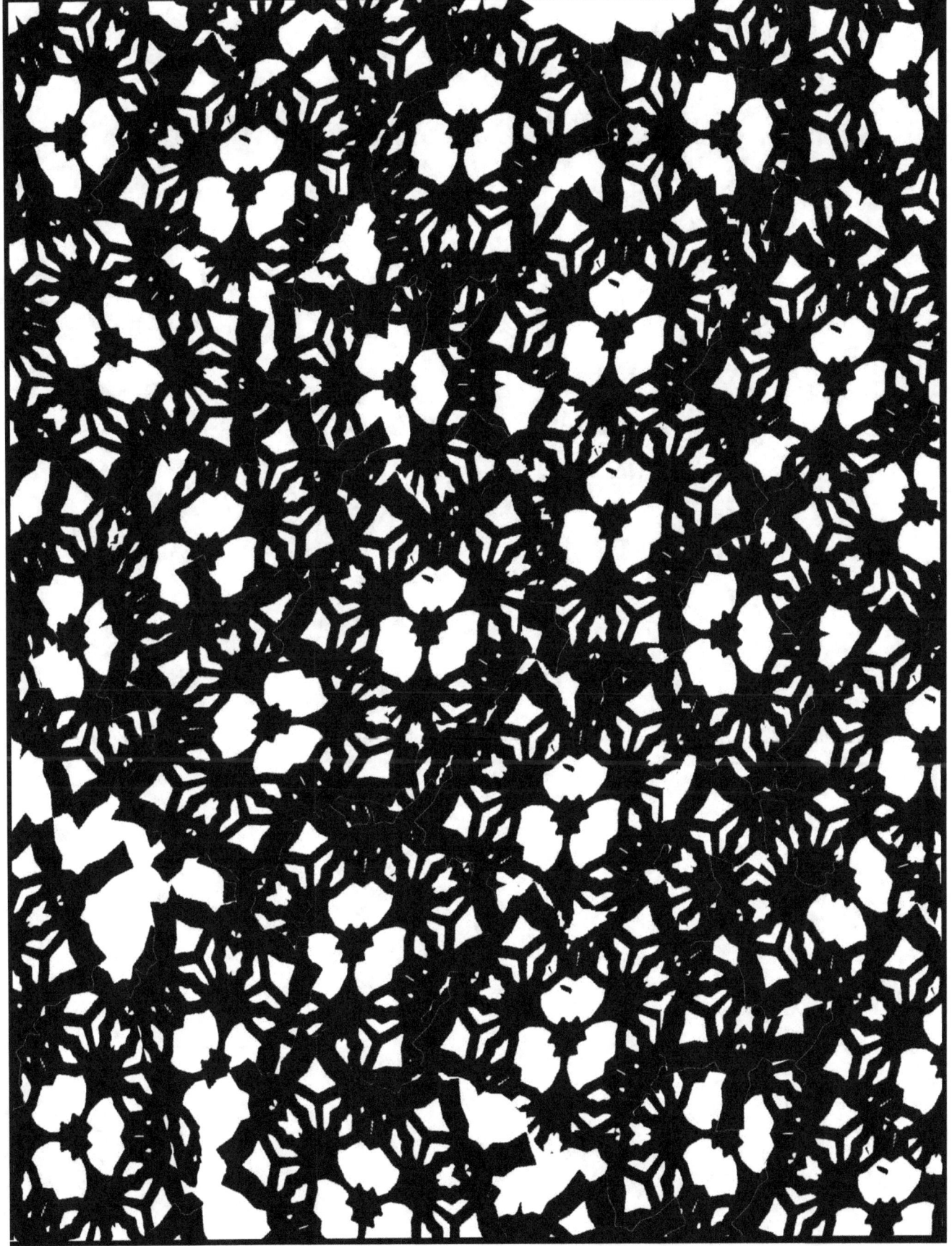

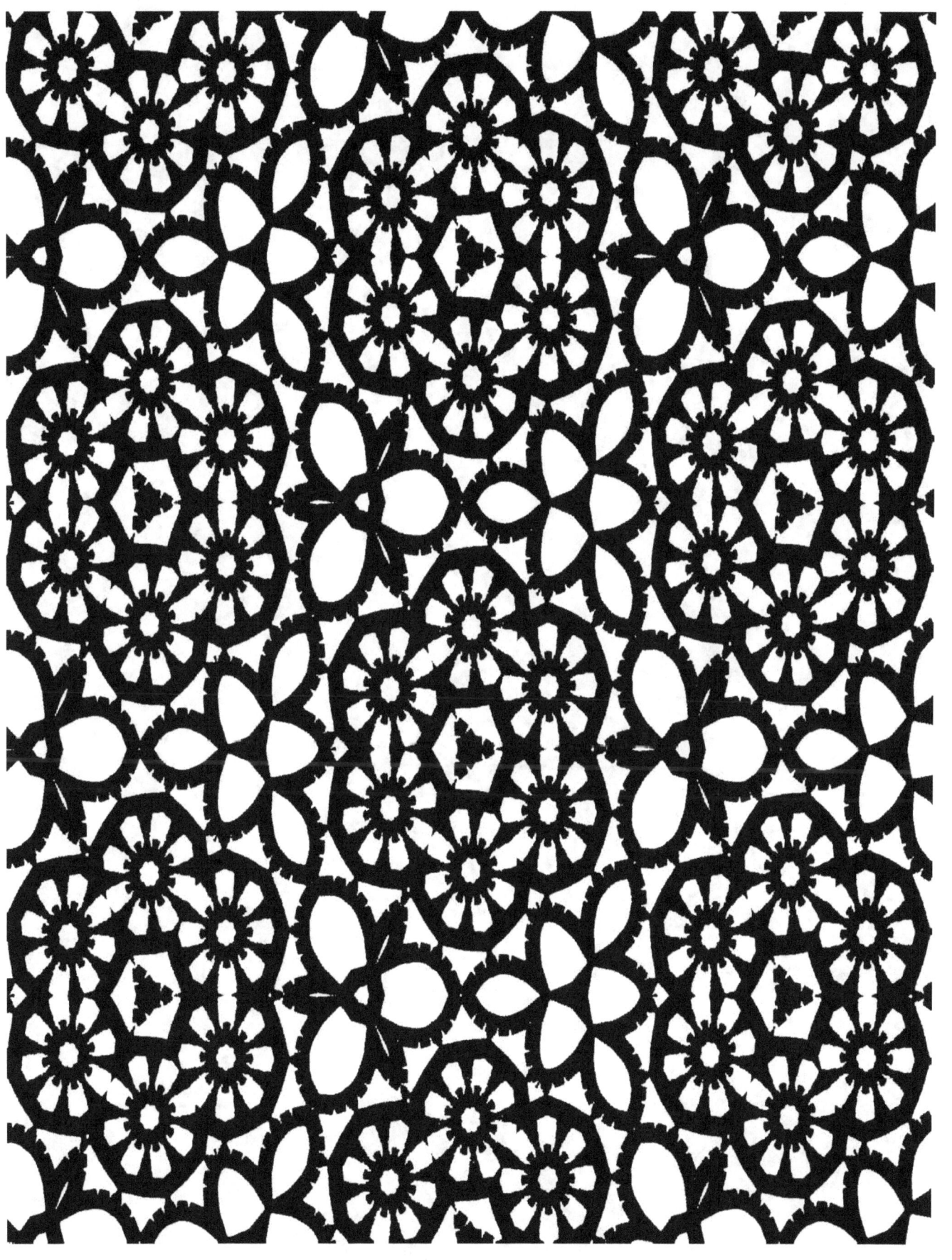

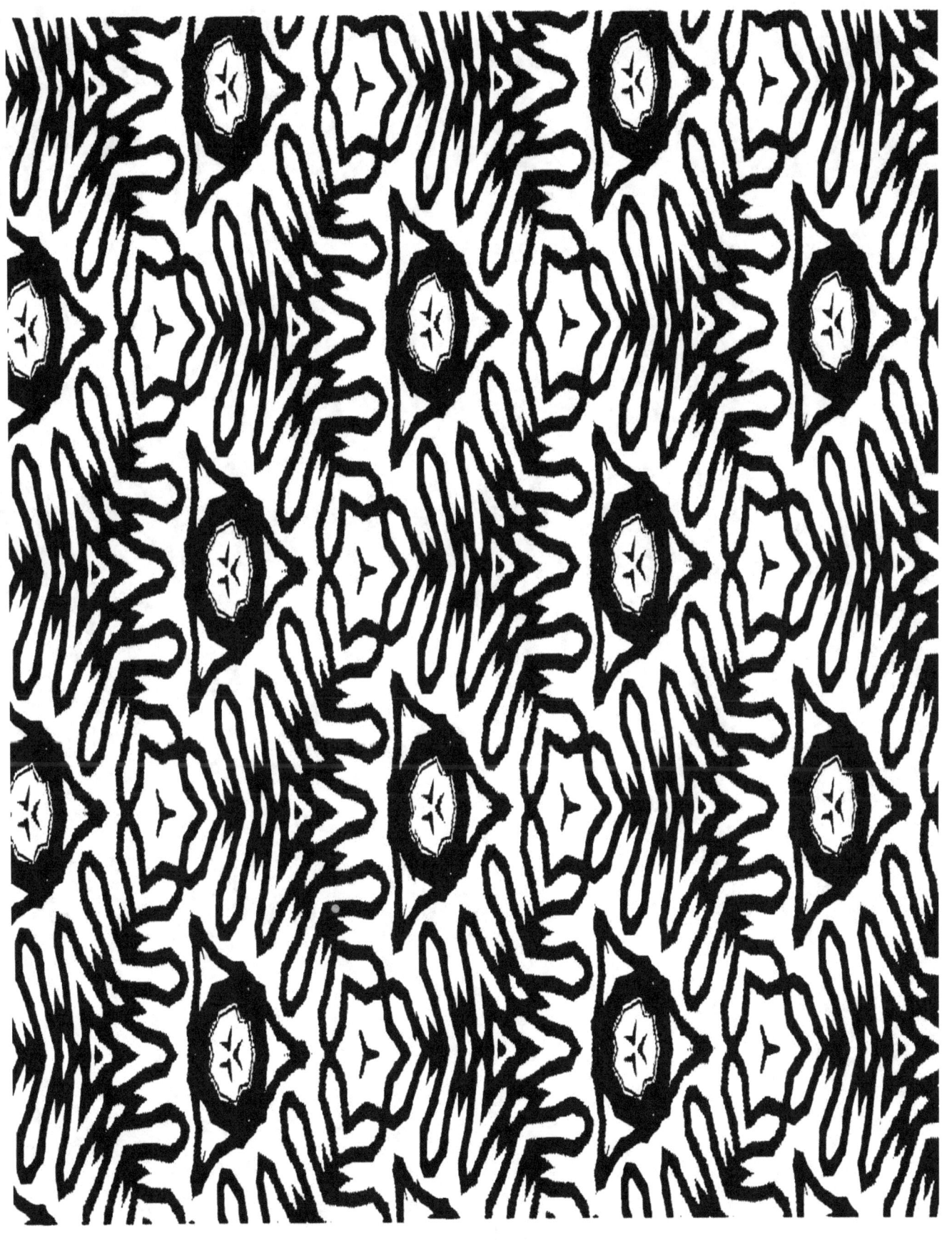

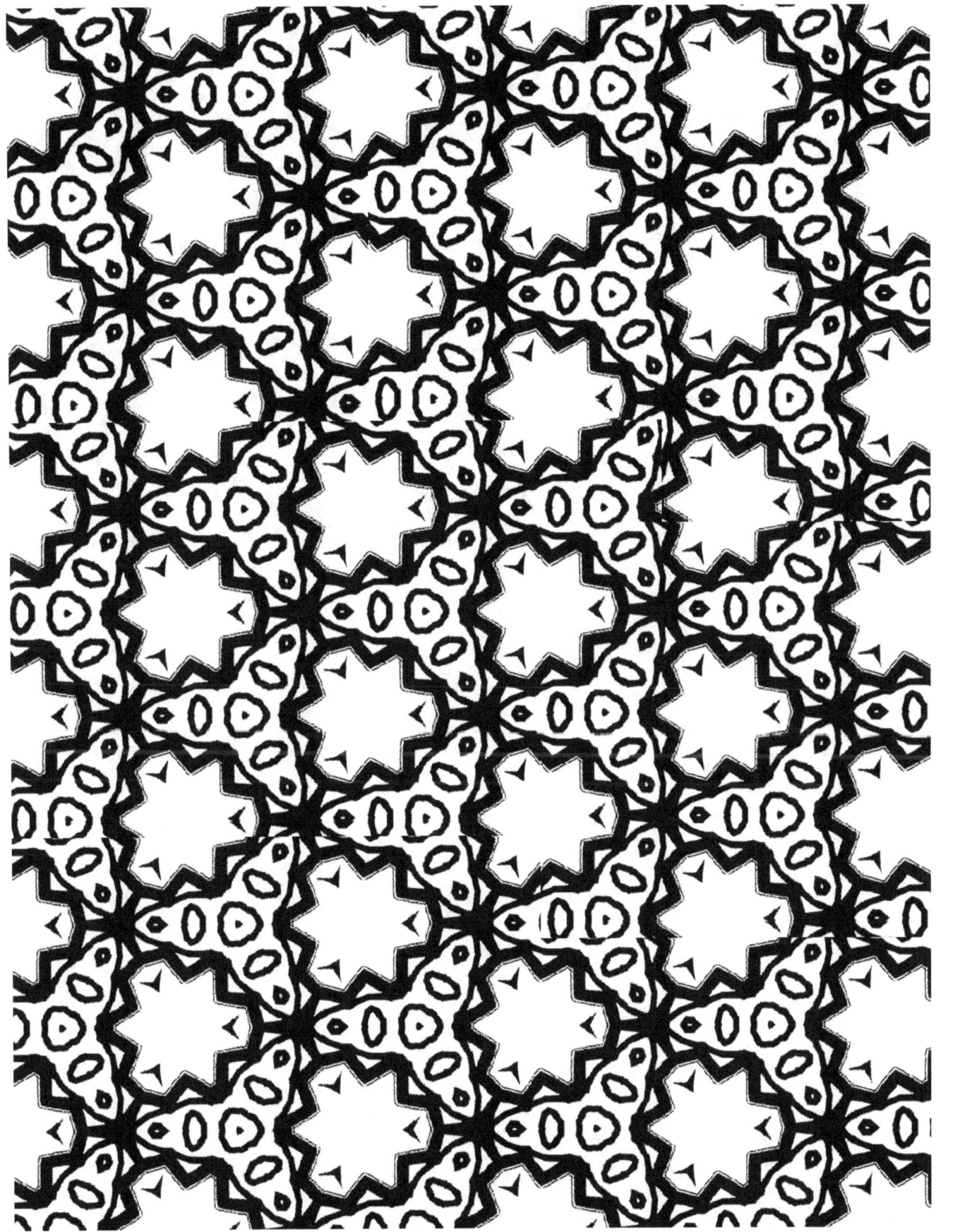

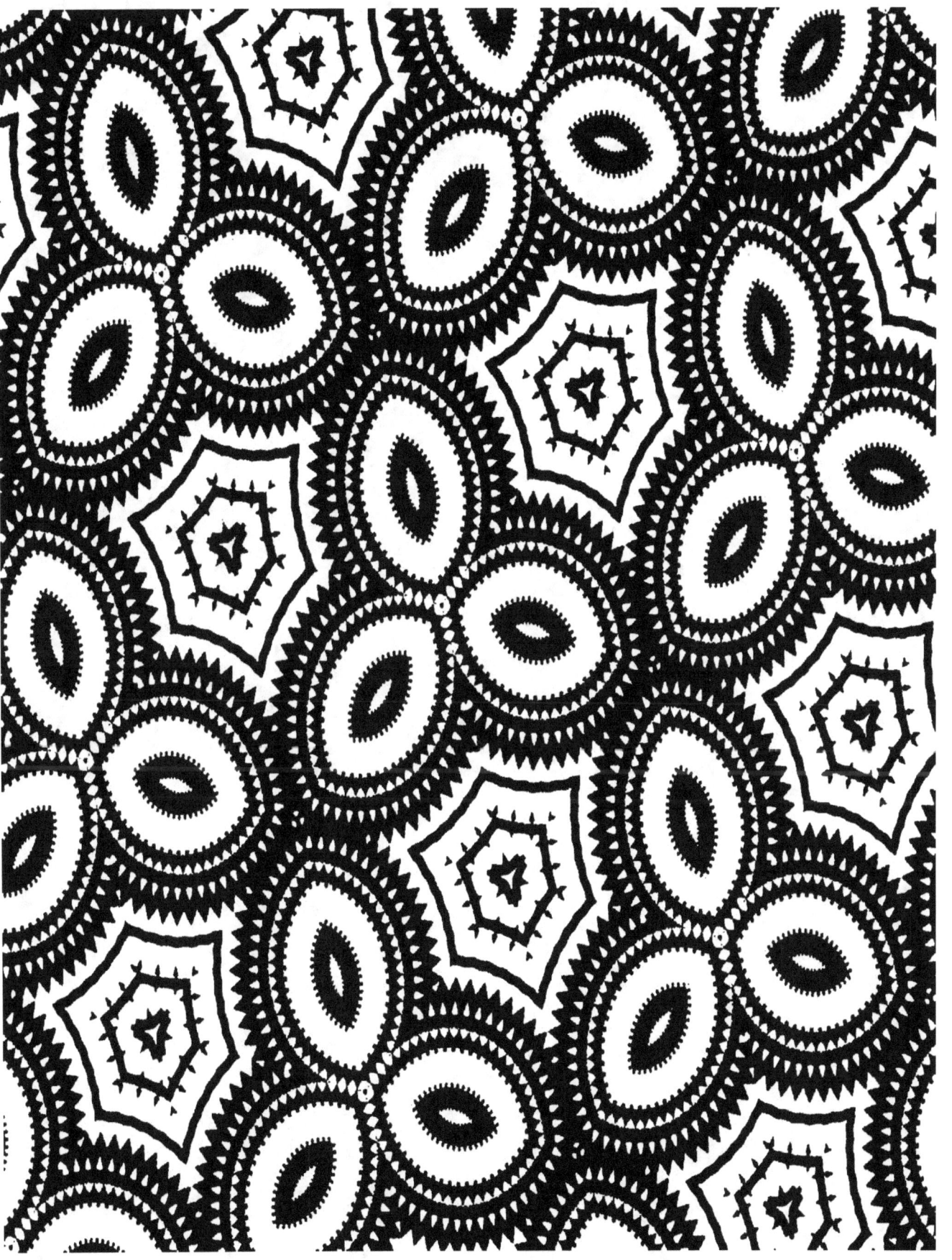

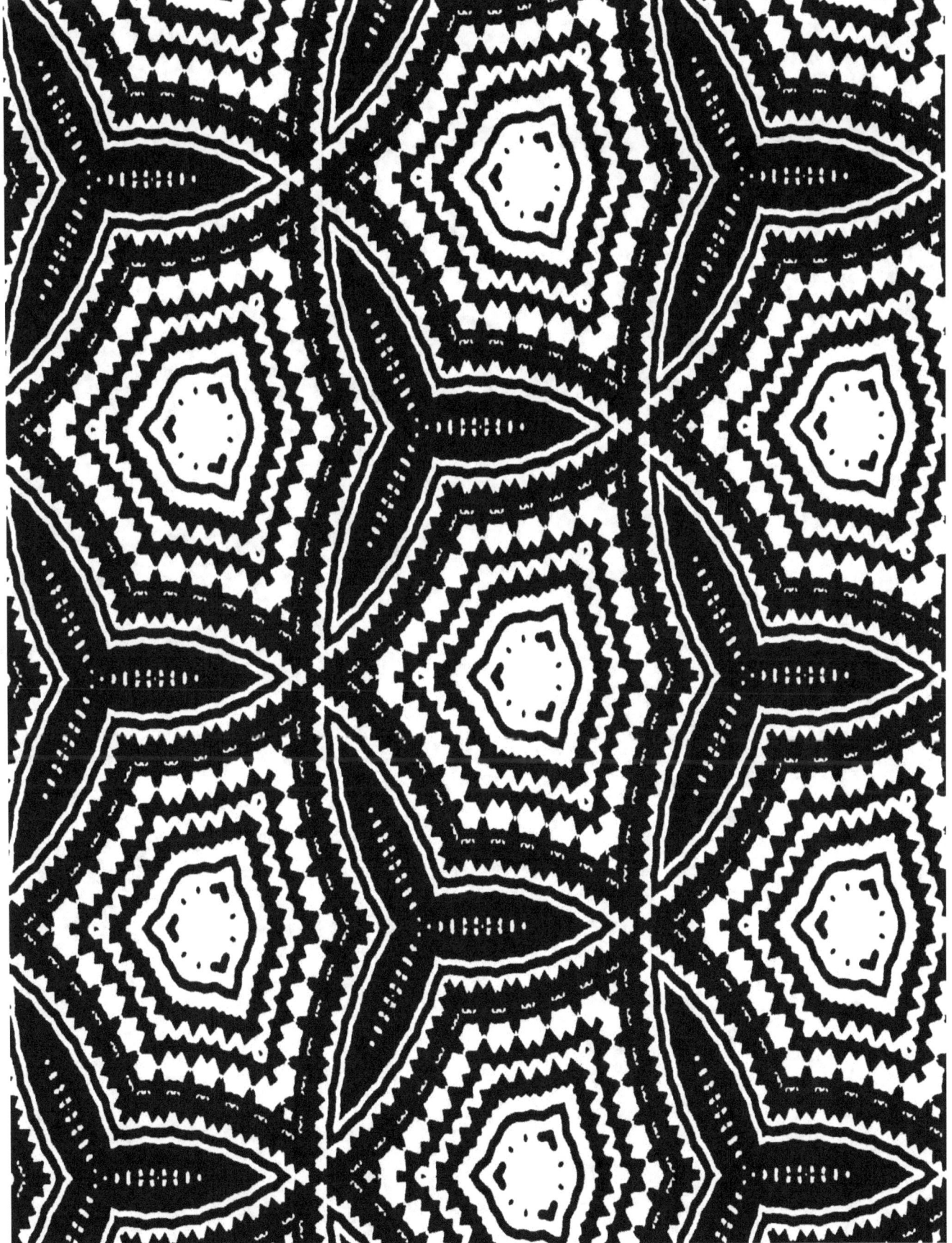

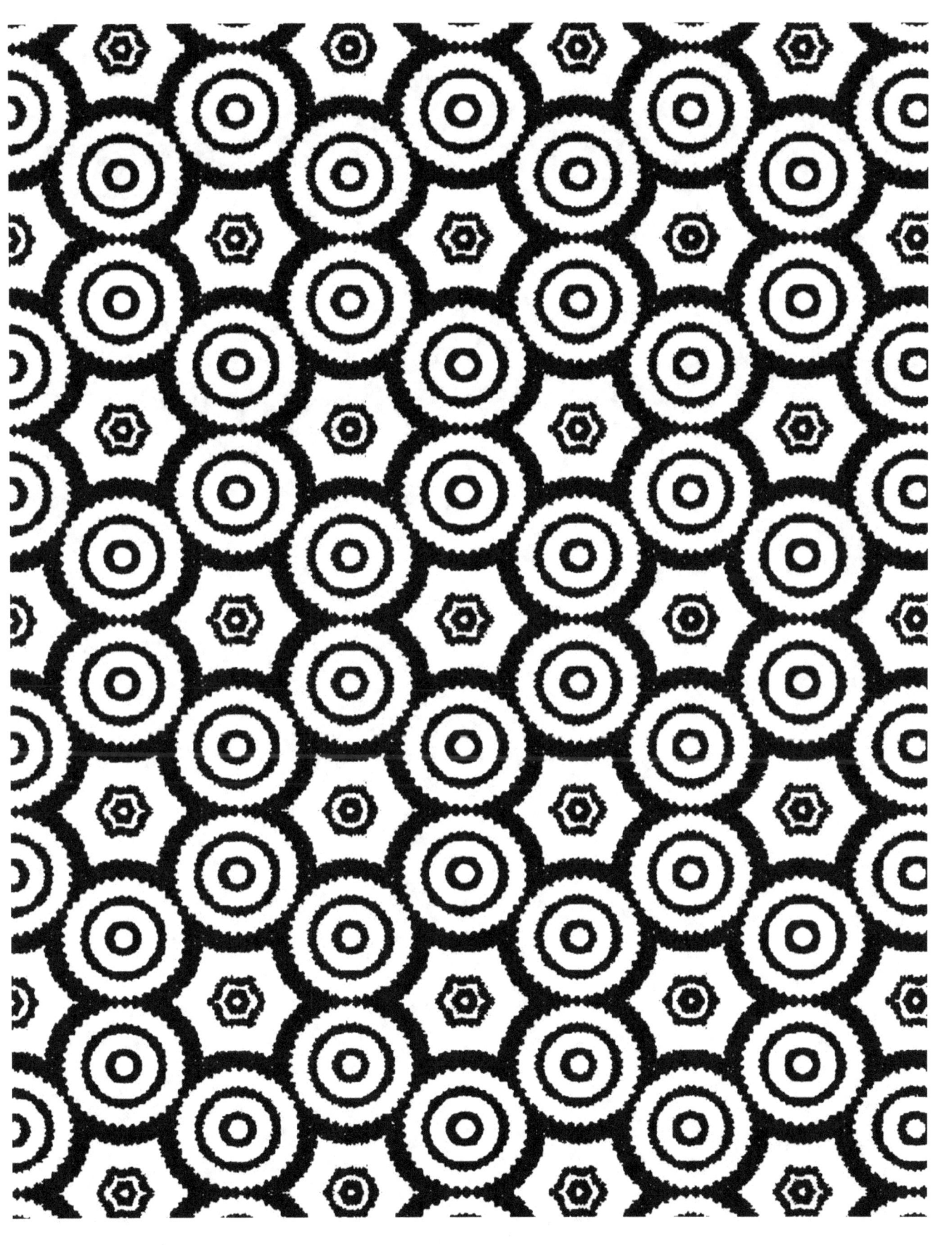

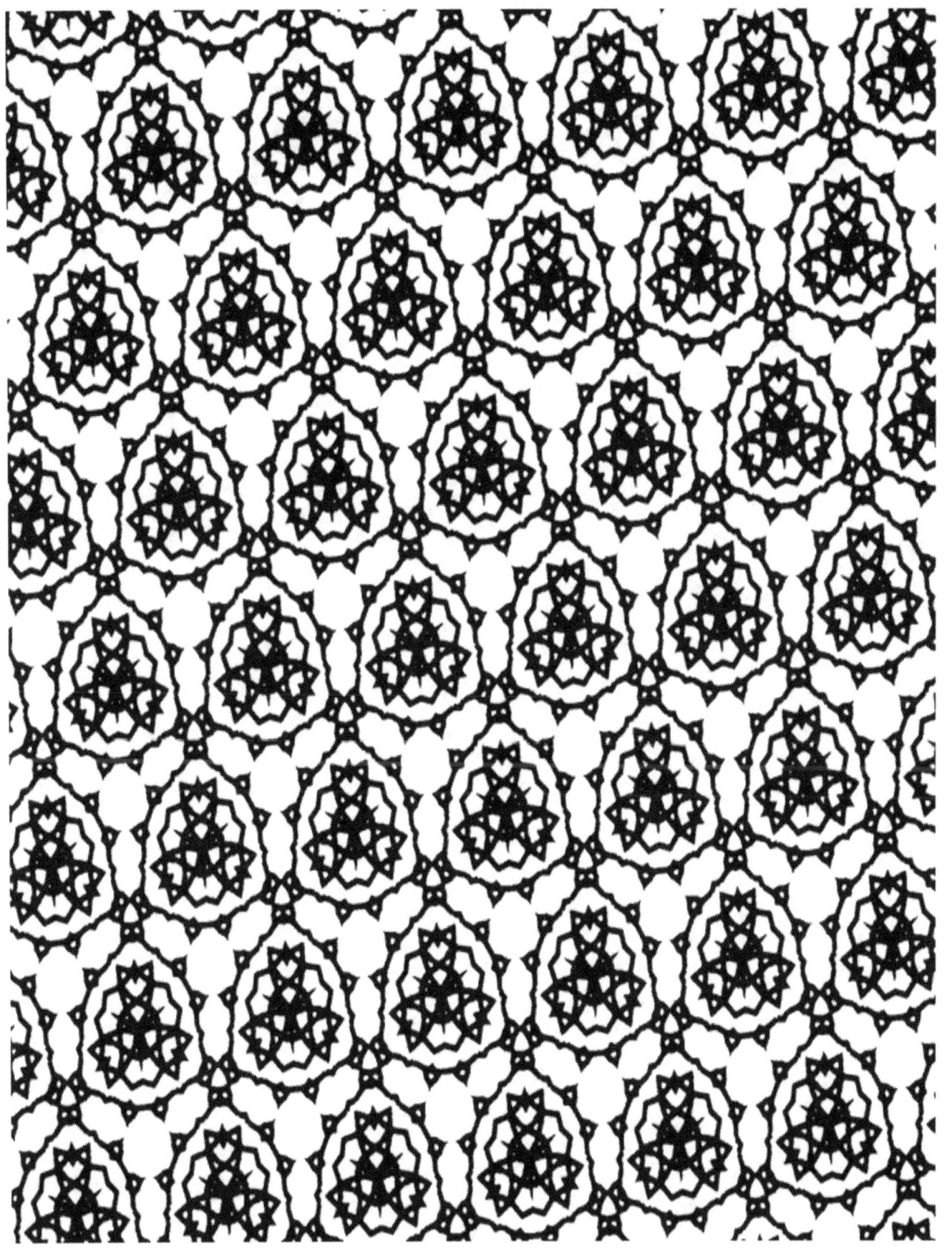

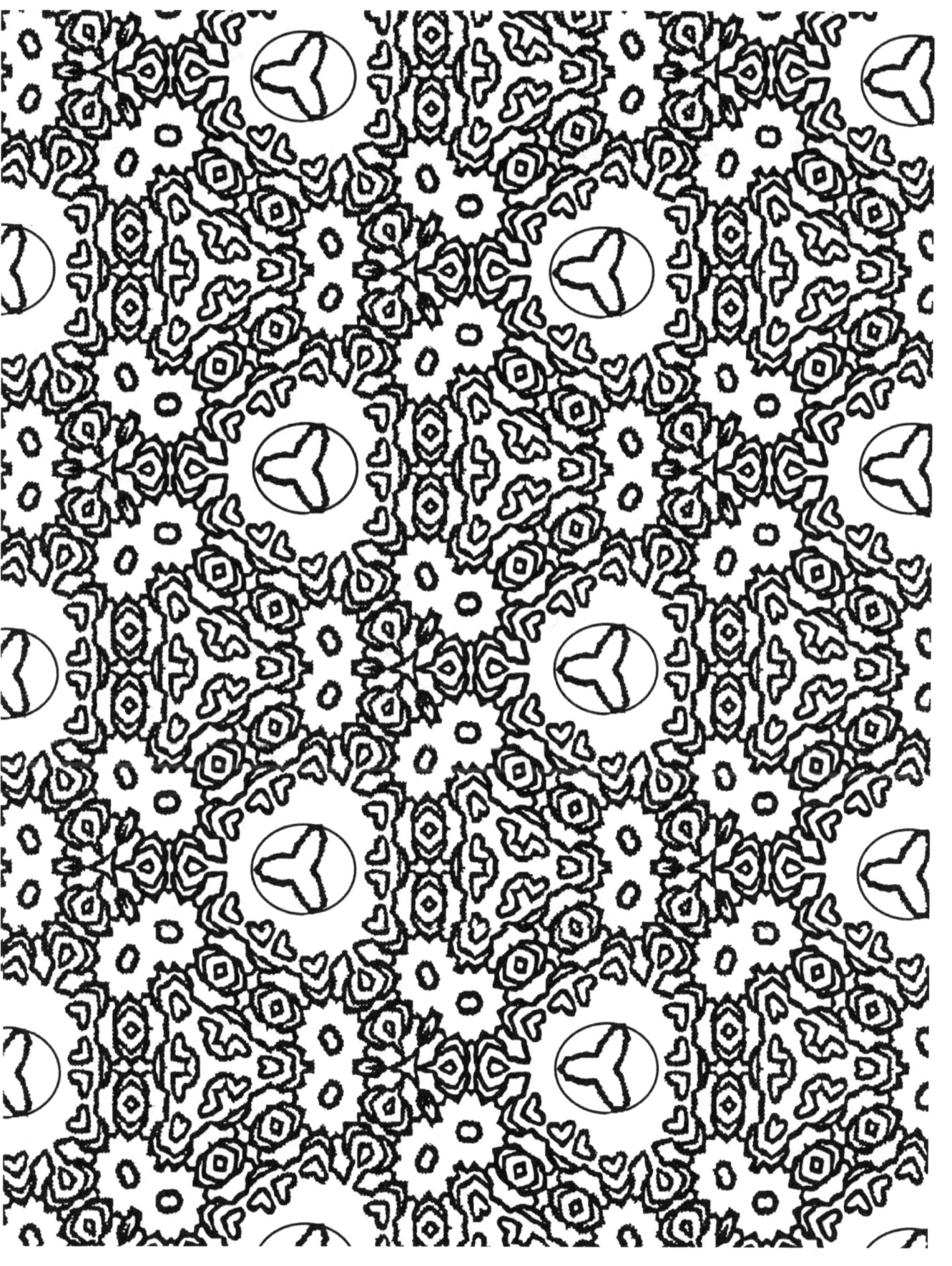

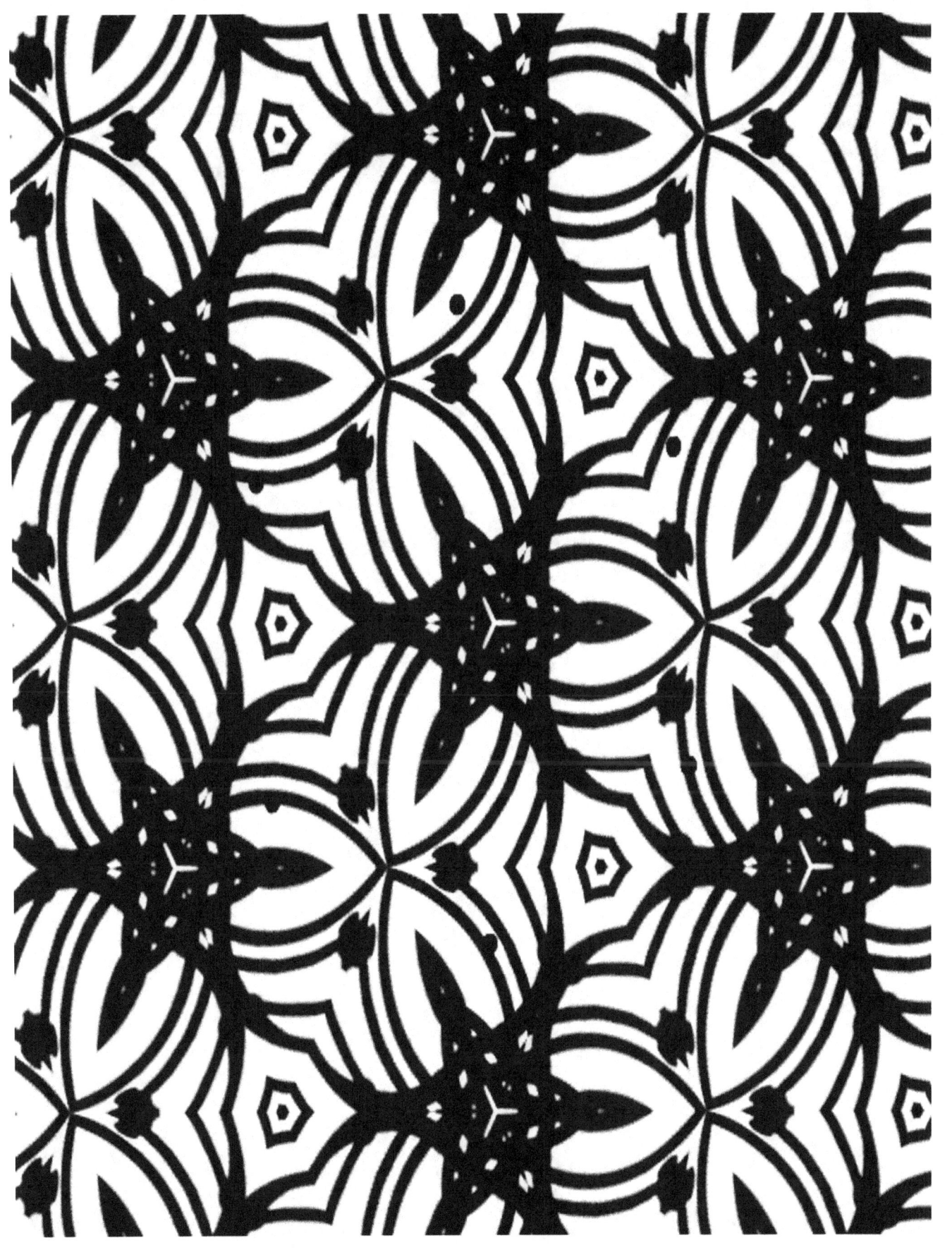

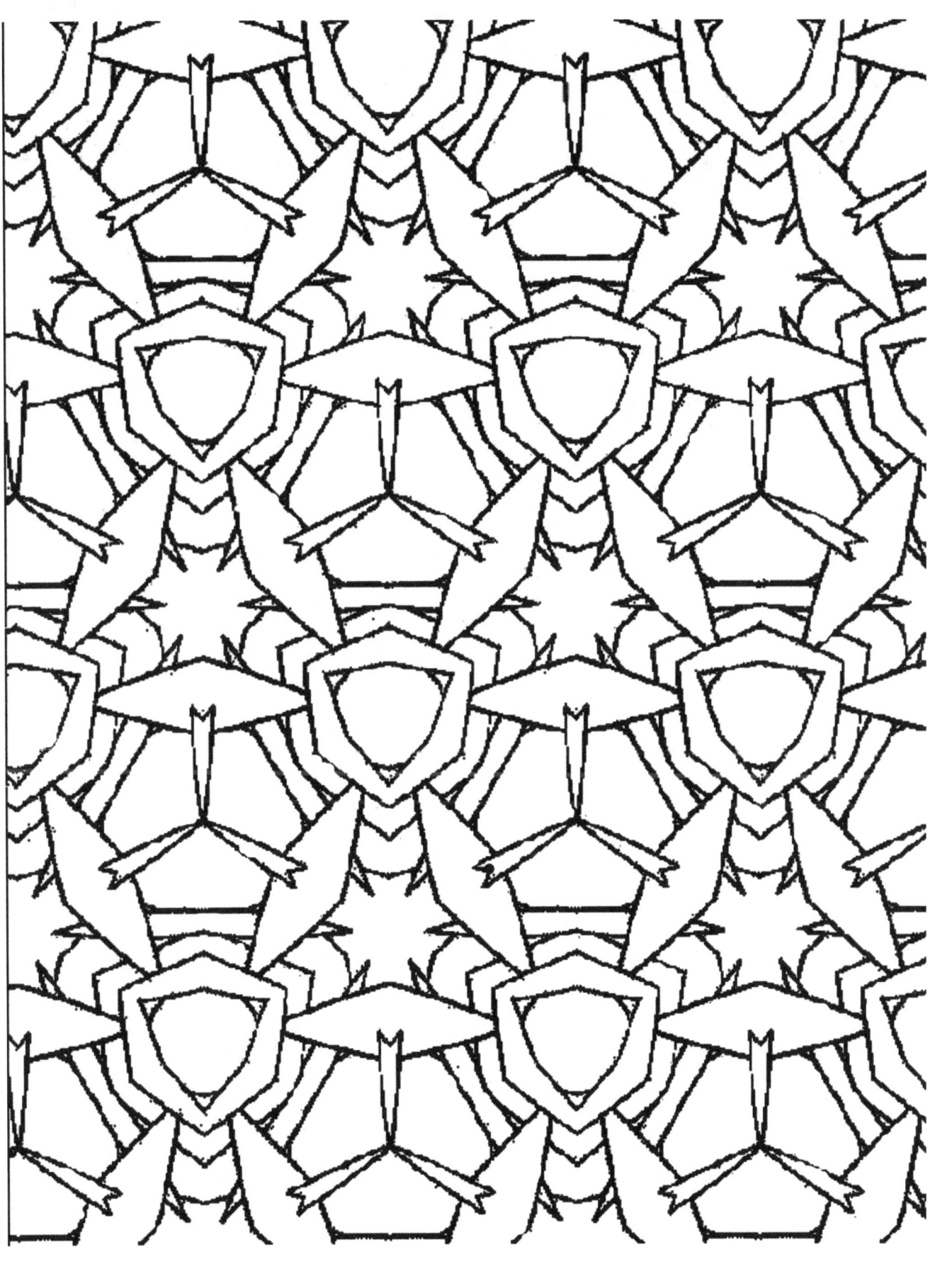

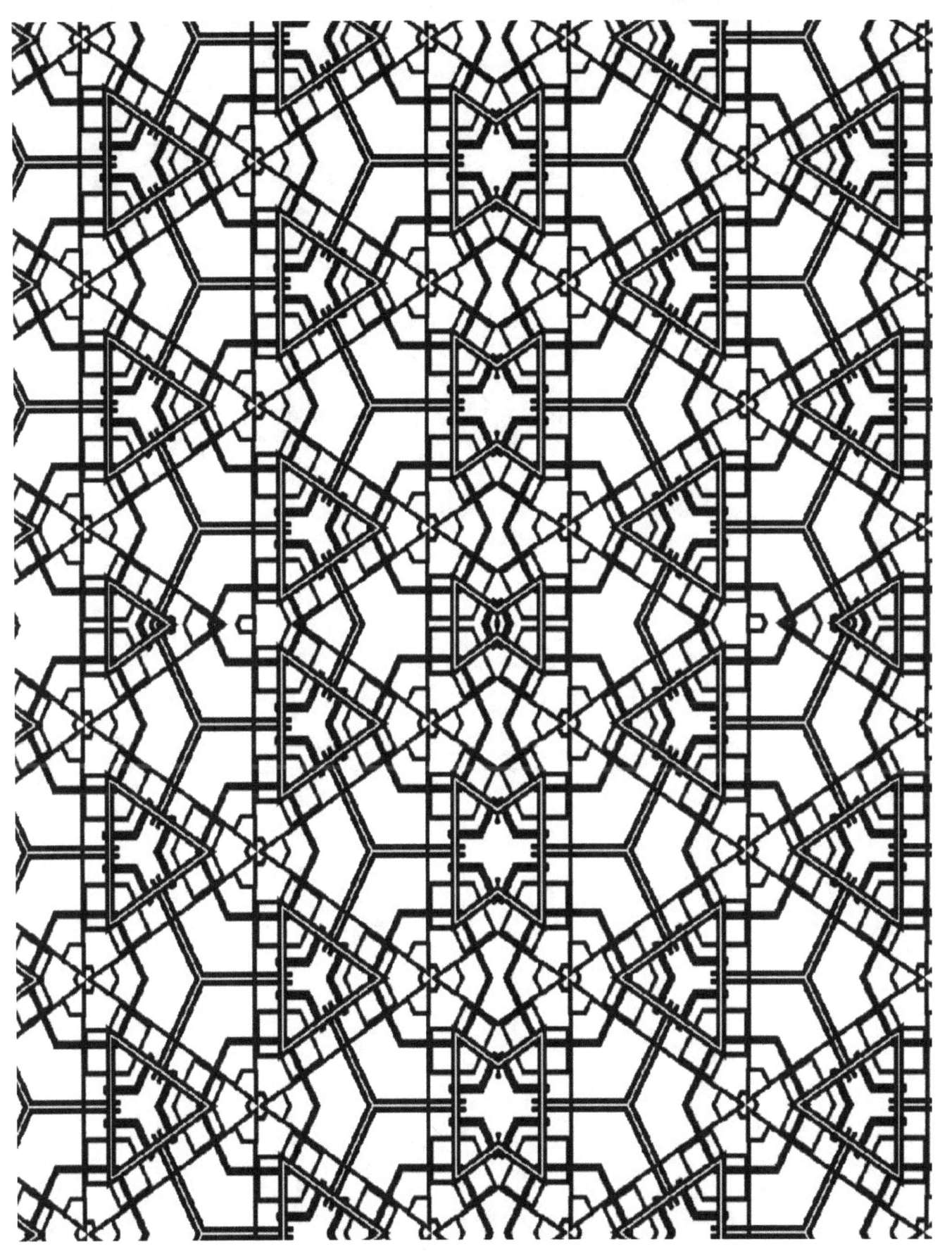

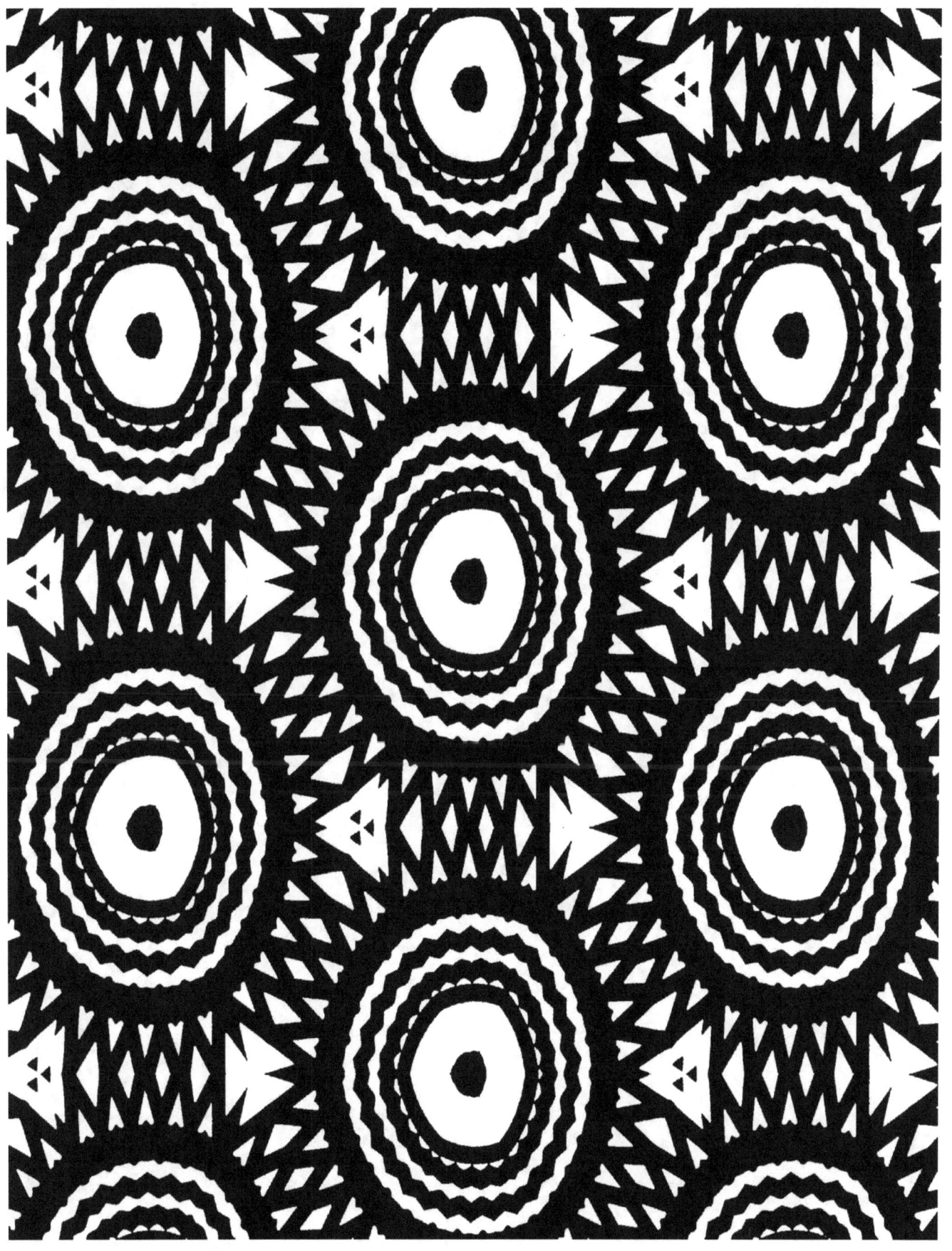

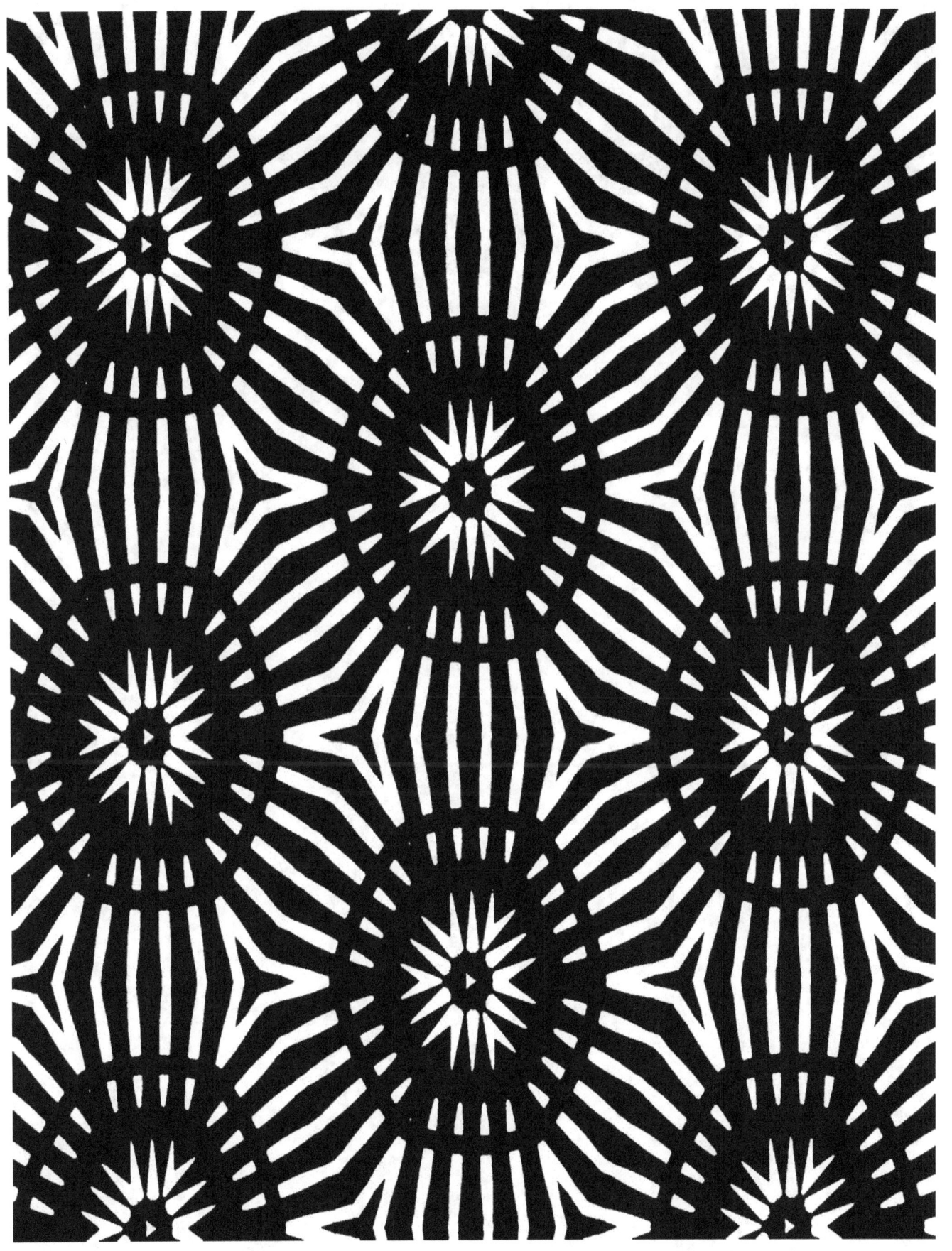

## Bonuses!

To thank you for purchasing *Pattern Perfect,* I'd like to offer you a couple of bonuses! (Yay! We all love bonuses!)

Swing by our Facebook page, give us a like and you'll receive a free image to color every couple of weeks. There will be periodic contests and it's a great place for you to show off your coloring genius! You'll find us at www.facebook.com/AdultColoringBookLovers, so you should have a pretty easy time remembering the address.

And, speaking of addresses, we have a website with all of our coloring books. The list is growing each week as Sherry Greywolf (my older sis) and I produce more images and compile them into books. We're having a blast and hope you will join us. The website will feature the books, yes, but we'll also try to throw in some interesting videos, blog posts from coloring experts, feature an image off our Facebook page and keep you as entertained as you can be without a colored pencil in your hands! Find us at AdultColoringBooks.weebly.com.

Thanks again for sharing your creativity with us!

Until next time,

*Nita*

(Debora Dyess)

www.ingramcontent.com/pod-product-compliance
Lightning Source LLC
Chambersburg PA
CBHW080826180526
45168CB00006B/2593